Why Men Love Strong and Independent Women

The Empowered Woman's Guide to Confidence, Assurance and Respect in a Relationship

Katie Wright

Copyright © 2024 by Katie Wright

All rights reserved. No part of this book may be reproduced, stored in a retrieval system, or transmitted in any form or by any means, electronic, mechanical, photocopying, recording, or otherwise, without prior written permission from the author, except for brief quotations in critical reviews or article

Table of Contents

Introduction	1
Chapter 1	11
The Power of Empowerment: Embracing Your Strength and Independence	11
The Essence of Empowerment	12
Embracing Your Strength	13
The Journey of Independence	14
The Attraction of Strength and Independence	19
Chapter 2	24
Confidence Unleashed: Building Self-Assurance and Self-Worth	24
Understanding Confidence	24
Practical Exercises for Building Confidence	29
The Impact of Confidence on Relationships	33
Chapter 3	38
Self-Discovery: Uncovering Your True Self and Values	38
The Importance of Self-Discovery	38
Uncovering Your Values	39
Enhancing Relationships Through Self-Discovery	44
Exercises for Self-Discovery	48
Chapter 4	52
Commanding Respect: Earning and Maintaining Respect in Relationships	52
Understanding the Dynamics of Respect	52
Earning Respect	55
Maintaining Respect	57

Exercises for Commanding and Maintaining Respect 61

Chapter 5   64
Celebrating Independence: The Beauty of Autonomy and Self-Sufficiency   64

Chapter 6   70
The Secrets of Attraction: Why Men Are Drawn to Strong Women   70

Chapter 7   78
Navigating Relationship Dynamics: Understanding Male-Female Interactions   78

Chapter 8   87
Mastering Communication: Effective Dialogue in Relationships   87

Chapter 9   97
Setting Healthy Boundaries: Maintaining Personal Space and Limits   97

Chapter 10   108
Nurturing Romance: Building and Sustaining Romantic Chemistry   108

- Understanding Romantic Chemistry   108
- The Power of Small Gestures   110
- Communication: The Heart of Romance   112
- The Importance of Trust and Honesty   117

Chapter 11   123
Personal Growth: Developing Your Passions and Interests   123

- The Importance of Personal Growth   123
- Balancing Individuality and Partnership   127
- Building Resilience and Emotional Intelligence   130

Seeking Mentorship and Guidance 132
Building Strong Support Network 134

Chapter 12   138
The Journey to Self-Love: Fostering Self-Acceptance and Care   138

Understanding Self-Love 138
Practices for Cultivating Self-Love 140
Overcoming Barriers to Self-Love 142
The Role of Self-Love in Relationships 144
The Journey to Self-Love 146

Chapter 13   150
The Romantic Paradox: Why Men Change Over Time 150

The Honeymoon Phase: A Period of Intense Romance 151
The Shift: Why Men May Change Over Time 152
Maintaining Romance and Connection 154
Understanding the Romantic Paradox 158

Chapter 14   161
The Nice Girl Syndrome: Avoiding Being Taken for Granted   161

Understanding the Nice Girl Syndrome 161
The Impact of Being Taken for Granted 163
Strategies to Assert Your Worth 165
Overcoming the Fear of Rejection 169
Building a Balanced and Respectful Relationship 170

Chapter 15   173
Earning Respect: The Strength of Standing Up for Yourself   173

The Importance of Respect in Relationships 173
Why Men Respect Women Who Stand Up for Themselves 175
Strategies to Command Respect 177
Overcoming Challenges to Standing Up for Yourself 180
The Benefits of Standing Up for Yourself 182

Chapter 16 **185**
Identifying Red Flags: Spotting Potential Pitfalls and Toxic Behaviors **185**
Understanding Red Flags and Their Importance 185
Common Red Flags in Relationships 187
Recognizing Subtle Red Flags 190
Tools for Identifying and Addressing Red Flags 192
Making Informed Decisions 194
Empowering Yourself with Knowledge and Awareness 196

Chapter 17 **198**
Building Healthy Relationships: Creating Fulfilling Partnerships **198**
The Foundation of Healthy Relationships 198
Building Emotional Intimacy 200
Effective Communication Strategies 201
Maintaining Mutual Respect 203
Cultivating Shared Goals and Values 204
Maintaining Romance and Passion 205
Navigating Challenges Together 207
Creating Fulfilling Partnerships 208

Conclusion **210**

Introduction

In a world where societal norms and expectations often dictate the dynamics of relationships, there is a growing need for a shift—a move towards empowerment, independence, and mutual respect. "Why Men Love Strong and Independent Women: The Empowered Woman's Guide to Confidence, Assurance, and Respect in Relationships" is more than just a book; it's a manifesto for every woman who has ever felt constrained by traditional roles and expectations. This book is a call to arms, an invitation to embrace your strength, independence, and individuality, and a roadmap to building fulfilling and balanced relationships.

The journey of writing this book has been one of deep reflection and passionate commitment. As a relationship counselor, I have had the privilege of working with countless women who, despite their incredible strength and potential, found themselves struggling in their romantic lives. They often faced the paradox of wanting to maintain their independence while also desiring meaningful, respectful partnerships. This struggle is not uncommon, and it is this very tension that inspired me to write this book.

Empowerment is not just a buzzword; it is the foundation of a fulfilled and meaningful life. It is the ability to recognize your worth, to stand tall in your truth, and to navigate the world with confidence and assurance. This book begins with the premise that every woman has the inherent power to shape her destiny, to command respect, and to inspire those around her. It is about understanding that true empowerment comes from within and manifests in how you carry yourself, the choices you make, and the relationships you cultivate.

One of the most alluring qualities a woman can possess is her strength and independence. Men are inherently drawn to women who exude confidence and are unapologetically themselves. This book delves into the psychology behind this attraction, exploring why strength and independence are not only desirable traits but essential ones for a healthy, balanced relationship.

By embracing your autonomy and self-sufficiency, you create a foundation of respect and admiration, paving the way for deeper, more meaningful connections.

The Journey of Self-Discovery

At the heart of every strong and independent woman is a deep understanding of herself. Self-discovery is a lifelong journey, one that requires introspection, honesty, and courage. This book guides you through this process, helping you uncover your values, passions, and desires. It is about peeling back the layers of societal conditioning and rediscovering the essence of who you are. When you truly know yourself, you can navigate relationships with clarity and authenticity, attracting partners who appreciate and celebrate your uniqueness.

Respect is the cornerstone of any successful relationship. It is earned, not demanded, and it is maintained through consistent actions and unwavering integrity. This book provides practical advice on how to command respect from men in your relationships. It explores the dynamics of respect, how it is communicated, and how it can be nurtured and preserved. By understanding the principles of respect, you can create a partnership that is balanced, fulfilling, and mutually respectful.

Independence is a beautiful and powerful quality. It is about being self-sufficient, making your own decisions, and living life on your terms. This book celebrates women's autonomy and provides insights into how to maintain and cultivate independence within the context of a relationship. It is about finding the balance between being in a partnership and retaining your individuality. Independence does not mean isolation; it means bringing your full, authentic self into the relationship and creating a dynamic that honors and respects both partners' autonomy.

Why are men attracted to strong, independent women? This book delves into the principles of attraction, uncovering the psychological and emotional factors that draw men to confident, self-assured women. It explores the power of presence, the allure of confidence, and the magnetic quality of authenticity. By understanding these principles, you can enhance your natural allure and create connections that are deep, genuine, and lasting.

Relationships are complex and multifaceted. This book provides a comprehensive exploration of relationship dynamics, helping you understand how men and women interact and relate to each other. It delves into the intricacies of communication, the importance of setting boundaries, and the role of emotional intelligence in building strong, healthy partnerships. By understanding these dynamics, you can navigate your relationships with grace and wisdom, fostering connections that are harmonious and fulfilling.

Communication is the lifeblood of any relationship. It is the bridge that connects hearts and minds, the conduit through which feelings and thoughts are expressed and understood. This book provides practical guidance on effective communication, helping you articulate your needs, listen actively, and respond empathetically. It explores the art of dialogue, the power of words, and the importance of non-verbal communication. By mastering these skills, you can create a deeper connection with your partner and foster a relationship built on understanding and mutual respect.

Boundaries are essential for maintaining personal space and protecting your well-being. This book explores the importance of setting healthy boundaries in relationships, providing practical advice on how to establish and maintain them. It is about understanding your limits, communicating them clearly, and respecting your partner's boundaries as well. By setting and maintaining healthy boundaries, you create a safe and respectful environment where both partners can thrive.

Romance is the spark that ignites the flame of love. It is the chemistry that draws two people together and creates a bond that is passionate and enduring. This book delves into the art of nurturing romantic chemistry, providing insights and advice on how to build and sustain a romantic connection with your partner. It explores the importance of intimacy, the role of playfulness, and the power of shared experiences. By nurturing romantic chemistry, you can create a relationship that is vibrant, passionate, and deeply fulfilling.

Personal growth and self-love are the foundations of a healthy and fulfilling life. This book encourages you to pursue your passions, develop your interests, and cultivate a strong sense of self-love and self-acceptance. It is about understanding that your relationship with yourself sets the tone for all other relationships in your life. By prioritizing personal growth and self-love, you create a foundation of strength and resilience that enhances every aspect of your life, including your romantic relationships.

One of the most puzzling aspects of relationships is the romantic paradox: why men can be intensely romantic at the beginning of a relationship but may change over time. This book explores this phenomenon, providing insights into the dynamics of romance and how to maintain it over the long term. It is about understanding the ebb and flow of romantic feelings and learning how to keep the spark alive in your relationship.

The Nice Girl Syndrome is a common trap that many women fall into, where they prioritize being nice and accommodating over asserting their needs and boundaries. This book explores why men often take nice girls for granted and provides strategies for avoiding this trap. It is about understanding the importance of standing up for yourself, asserting your worth, and maintaining a balance between kindness and self-respect.

Respect is earned through consistent actions, integrity, and self-assuredness. This book provides practical advice on how to earn and command respect in your relationships. It explores the dynamics of respect, how it is communicated, and how it can be nurtured and preserved. By understanding the principles of respect, you can create a partnership that is balanced, fulfilling, and mutually respectful.

Relationships can be fraught with potential pitfalls and red flags. This book provides tools and insights to help you identify and navigate these challenges. It is about recognizing toxic behaviors, understanding the signs of unhealthy dynamics, and making informed decisions about your relationships. By being aware of potential red flags, you can protect yourself and build relationships that are healthy and fulfilling.

Ultimately, the goal of this book is to help you build healthy, fulfilling relationships based on mutual respect, love, and understanding. It provides a comprehensive guide to creating and nurturing strong partnerships, offering practical advice, insights, and strategies to help you navigate the complexities of modern relationships. By embracing your strength, independence, and individuality, you can create relationships that are not only successful but deeply fulfilling.

As you embark on this journey, remember that you are not alone. Every woman has the potential to be strong, independent, and empowered. It is my hope that this book will serve as a guiding light, inspiring you to embrace your true self, command respect, and build relationships that are worthy of you. Your strength is your greatest asset, and your independence is your most powerful tool. Together, they create a force that is irresistible, inspiring, and profoundly impactful.

Welcome to "Why Men Love Strong and Independent Women: The Empowered Woman's Guide to Confidence, Assurance, and Respect in Relationships." This is your journey to empowerment, your guide to building meaningful connections, and your manifesto for living a life of confidence, assurance, and respect.

Chapter 1

The Power of Empowerment: Embracing Your Strength and Independence

Empowerment is not just a buzzword; it's a transformative journey that reshapes your identity and relationships. Embracing your strength and independence isn't merely about projecting an image of confidence to the outside world—it's about fundamentally altering the way you perceive yourself, interact with others, and navigate life's challenges. It therefore looks into the deep-seated power of empowerment, illustrating how embracing your strength and independence can lead to personal fulfillment and attract meaningful relationships.

The Essence of Empowerment

Empowerment begins with a profound understanding of your inherent worth. It's about recognizing that you have the right to pursue your dreams, set your boundaries, and demand respect. This realization often requires unlearning societal expectations that dictate how women should behave. From a young age, many women are taught to prioritize others' needs over their own, to be nurturing and accommodating, often at the expense of their own desires and well-being. Empowerment challenges these norms by encouraging women to prioritize their own happiness and well-being.

At its core, empowerment is about self-ownership. It's the recognition that you are the master of your own destiny, capable of making choices that reflect your true self. This doesn't mean that you won't face obstacles or that you won't need support from others. Rather, it means that you approach life's challenges with a sense of agency and resilience, confident in your ability to overcome adversity.

Embracing Your Strength

Strength manifests in various forms—emotional, mental, physical, and spiritual. Embracing your strength means acknowledging and cultivating these aspects within yourself. Emotional strength involves resilience, the ability to bounce back from setbacks, and maintain a positive outlook despite challenges. It's about understanding that vulnerability and strength are not mutually exclusive; showing your true self, including your fears and doubts, can be a profound act of strength.

Mental strength is about cultivating a mindset that embraces growth and learning. It's the capacity to face challenges head-on, to think critically, and to make decisions that align with your values. Developing mental strength involves continuous learning, seeking new experiences, and challenging yourself to step outside your comfort zone.

Physical strength is often overlooked in discussions of empowerment, but it plays a crucial role in how you perceive yourself and how others perceive you. Engaging in physical activities, whether it's exercise, sports, or yoga, can significantly boost your confidence and energy levels. Physical strength is not about achieving a specific body type but about feeling capable and strong in your own skin.

Spiritual strength involves connecting with your inner self and understanding your place in the world. It's about finding a sense of purpose and meaning in life, which can provide immense strength and resilience during tough times. Practices like meditation, mindfulness, or engaging in religious or spiritual activities can help cultivate this inner strength.

The Journey of Independence

Independence is the ability to live your life according to your own terms. It's about having the freedom to make your own choices and the confidence to pursue your goals without relying on others for validation or support. Independence doesn't mean isolation; it's about interdependence, where you can stand on your own while also forming healthy, supportive relationships.

Financial independence is a critical aspect of overall independence. It provides the freedom to make choices without being constrained by financial dependence on others. Achieving financial independence involves managing your finances wisely, understanding your economic worth, and planning for the future. It's about making informed decisions that support your long-term goals and security.

Emotional independence is equally important. It's the ability to regulate your emotions and not depend on others for your sense of self-worth or happiness. Emotional independence involves setting healthy boundaries, recognizing toxic relationships, and knowing when to walk away from situations that do not serve your well-being.

Individuality: The Unique You

Your individuality is what sets you apart from everyone else. Embracing your individuality means celebrating your unique traits, talents, and perspectives. It's about being unapologetically yourself, without feeling the need to conform to societal expectations or the opinions of others.

Individuality is closely linked to authenticity. When you embrace your true self, you attract people who appreciate you for who you are, rather than a facade you might present. Authenticity fosters genuine connections and deepens relationships, as it allows others to see and appreciate your true self.

Empowerment in Action

The journey to empowerment involves actionable steps that integrate strength, independence, and individuality into your daily life. Here are some strategies to help you embrace these qualities:

Self-Reflection and Self-Awareness

Regularly take time to reflect on your values, goals, and desires. Understand what truly matters to you and what you want to achieve in life. Self-awareness is the foundation of empowerment, as it helps you make decisions that align with your true self.

Setting Boundaries

Learn to set and maintain healthy boundaries. This involves saying no to things that don't serve your well-being and yes to things that do. Boundaries protect your emotional and physical space, allowing you to focus on your priorities and maintain your independence.
Continuous Learning

Invest in your personal and professional growth. Whether it's through formal education, online courses, or self-study, continuous learning helps you build mental strength and stay adaptable in a rapidly changing world.

Financial Management

Take control of your finances by budgeting, saving, and investing wisely. Financial independence is a cornerstone of overall independence, providing you with the freedom to make choices that align with your goals.

Physical Health

Prioritize your physical health through regular exercise, a balanced diet, and adequate rest. Physical strength enhances your confidence and energy levels, enabling you to tackle challenges more effectively.

Emotional Regulation

Develop skills to manage your emotions, such as mindfulness, meditation, or therapy. Emotional independence allows you to maintain your sense of self-worth and happiness, regardless of external circumstances.

Authentic Relationships

Build relationships that are based on mutual respect, trust, and authenticity. Surround yourself with people who support your growth and celebrate your individuality.

Pursuing Passions

Engage in activities and hobbies that bring you joy and fulfillment. Pursuing your passions helps you stay connected to your true self and enhances your overall sense of well-being.

The Attraction of Strength and Independence

One of the key themes of this book is understanding why men are drawn to strong, independent women. The answer lies in the qualities that empowerment fosters—confidence, self-assuredness, and authenticity. These traits are inherently attractive because they signal a sense of self-worth and the ability to contribute positively to a relationship.

Men, like women, seek partners who are confident in themselves and who bring positivity and strength to the relationship. A strong, independent woman is seen as a partner who can stand on her own, support her partner, and contribute to a balanced and fulfilling relationship. This dynamic creates a foundation of mutual respect and admiration, which is essential for a healthy, lasting partnership.

Personal Fulfillment and Happiness

Beyond attraction, embracing your strength and independence leads to personal fulfillment and happiness. When you live according to your true self, you experience a deeper sense of satisfaction and joy. Empowerment allows you to pursue your dreams, build meaningful relationships, and navigate life's challenges with confidence and resilience.

Personal fulfillment comes from living a life that aligns with your values and passions. It's about setting goals that reflect your true desires and taking steps to achieve them. When you embrace your strength and independence, you create a life that is rich in meaning and purpose, fostering a sense of happiness that is rooted in authenticity.

Real-Life Scenarios

To illustrate the power of empowerment, let's consider some real-life scenarios:

The Career Woman

Sarah is a successful career woman who has always prioritized her professional growth. She has faced numerous challenges in a male-dominated industry but has consistently risen to the occasion. By embracing her strength and independence, Sarah has not only advanced in her career but also attracted a partner who respects and admires her drive and determination. Their relationship is built on mutual support and shared goals, creating a balanced and fulfilling partnership.

The Single Mother

Emily is a single mother who has navigated the challenges of raising her child while pursuing her education and career. By embracing her independence, Emily has built a stable and fulfilling life for herself and her child. Her strength and resilience have attracted a partner who values her dedication and supports her in her journey. Their relationship is based on mutual respect and admiration, creating a strong foundation for their family.

The Passionate Artist

Lena is an artist who has always followed her passion for painting. Despite societal pressure to pursue a more conventional career, Lena has remained true to herself. By embracing her individuality and independence, she has built a successful career as an artist and attracted a partner who appreciates her creativity and uniqueness. Their relationship is vibrant and passionate, fueled by their shared love for the arts.

Empowerment is a journey that transforms every aspect of your life. By embracing your strength, independence, and individuality, you not only attract meaningful relationships but also foster personal fulfillment and happiness. This chapter has explored the essence of empowerment, the journey of embracing your strength and independence, and the impact it has on your life and relationships.

Chapter 2

Confidence Unleashed: Building Self-Assurance and Self-Worth

Confidence is a powerful force that shapes our lives, our relationships, and our futures. It's the invisible thread that weaves through every interaction, every decision, and every step we take toward our dreams. We will explore the transformative power of confidence and provide practical tips and exercises to help you build self-assurance and cultivate a strong sense of self-worth.

Understanding Confidence

Confidence is not an innate trait that only a lucky few possess. It is a skill that can be learned, developed, and strengthened over time. At its core, confidence is about believing in your abilities and trusting yourself to handle whatever comes your way. It's the assurance that you can face challenges, take risks, and achieve your goals.

Many people mistakenly believe that confidence is about being extroverted or always knowing the right answer. However, true confidence is more about how you feel about yourself and less about how you appear to others. It's the quiet inner strength that allows you to stand firm in your beliefs, values, and decisions.

The Foundation of Self-Worth

Before we dive into building confidence, it's crucial to understand the foundation of self-worth. Self-worth is the deep-seated belief that you are valuable, deserving of love, and worthy of respect. It's the internal acknowledgment of your inherent worth, regardless of external achievements or validation.

A strong sense of self-worth is the bedrock upon which confidence is built. Without it, confidence can become fragile and dependent on external factors. Cultivating self-worth involves recognizing your intrinsic value and treating yourself with kindness, compassion, and respect.

Overcoming Self-Doubt

Self-doubt is one of the biggest obstacles to building confidence. It's the inner voice that questions your abilities, undermines your achievements, and magnifies your fears. Overcoming self-doubt requires a conscious effort to challenge and reframe these negative thoughts.

Start by identifying the sources of your self-doubt. Often, these doubts stem from past experiences, societal expectations, or critical feedback from others. Once you recognize where these doubts come from, you can begin to address them.

One effective strategy is to counteract negative self-talk with positive affirmations. Replace thoughts like "I'm not good enough" with "I am capable and deserving of success." It may feel awkward at first, but with practice, positive affirmations can help rewire your brain to focus on your strengths and achievements.

Building Self-Assurance

Self-assurance is the confidence that comes from knowing and trusting yourself. It's the belief that you have the skills, knowledge, and resilience to navigate life's challenges. Building self-assurance involves both internal and external practices.

Set Achievable Goals

Start by setting small, achievable goals that align with your interests and values. Accomplishing these goals will provide a sense of accomplishment and reinforce your belief in your abilities. As you achieve these smaller goals, gradually set more challenging ones to continue building your confidence.

Develop Competence

Confidence grows from competence. Invest time in developing your skills and knowledge in areas that matter to you. Whether it's through formal education, online courses, or self-study, continuous learning helps you feel more capable and confident in your abilities.

Take Risks

Confidence often requires stepping outside your comfort zone. Take calculated risks and embrace new experiences. Each time you face a fear or challenge, you build resilience and strengthen your self-assurance. Remember, growth happens when you push beyond your perceived limits.

Celebrate Successes

Acknowledge and celebrate your achievements, no matter how small. Take time to reflect on your progress and give yourself credit for your hard work and dedication. Celebrating successes reinforces positive behavior and boosts your confidence.

Learn from Failures

Failure is an inevitable part of the journey to building confidence. Instead of viewing failure as a setback, see it as a learning opportunity. Analyze what went wrong, extract valuable lessons, and use them to improve. Resilience is built by bouncing back from failures with a stronger resolve.

Practical Exercises for Building Confidence

To help you build confidence, here are some practical exercises that you can incorporate into your daily routine:

Visualization

Visualization is a powerful technique that involves imagining yourself succeeding in various situations. Spend a few minutes each day visualizing yourself achieving your goals, handling challenges with ease, and exuding confidence. Visualization helps program your mind for success and boosts your self-assurance.

Journaling

Keeping a journal can help you track your progress, reflect on your experiences, and gain insights into your thoughts and feelings. Write about your achievements, challenges, and the steps you're taking to build confidence. Journaling provides a safe space to explore your emotions and reinforce positive changes.

Positive Affirmations

As mentioned earlier, positive affirmations are a great way to counteract negative self-talk. Create a list of affirmations that resonate with you, such as "I am confident and capable," "I deserve success and happiness," or "I trust myself to make the right decisions." Repeat these affirmations daily to reinforce your self-belief.

Body Language

Your body language has a significant impact on how you feel about yourself and how others perceive you. Practice confident body language by standing tall, maintaining eye contact, and using open, assertive gestures. Adopting a confident posture can boost your self-assurance and influence how others respond to you.

Mindfulness and Meditation

Mindfulness and meditation can help you stay present, reduce anxiety, and cultivate a sense of inner calm. Practice mindfulness by focusing on your breath, observing your thoughts without judgment, and staying grounded in the present moment. Regular meditation can enhance your self-awareness and strengthen your confidence.

Cultivating Self-Worth

Building confidence goes hand-in-hand with cultivating self-worth. Here are some strategies to help you recognize and embrace your intrinsic value:

Self-Compassion

Treat yourself with the same kindness and compassion that you would offer a friend. Acknowledge your struggles, forgive your mistakes, and give yourself permission to be imperfect. Self-compassion fosters a nurturing relationship with yourself and enhances your self-worth.

Boundaries

Setting and maintaining healthy boundaries is essential for protecting your self-worth. Learn to say no to things that don't align with your values or drain your energy. Respect your own needs and prioritize your well-being.

Boundaries help you maintain your sense of self and prevent others from undermining your worth.

Surround Yourself with Positivity

Surround yourself with people who uplift, support, and inspire you. Positive relationships reinforce your self-worth and provide a nurturing environment for growth. Distance yourself from toxic individuals who undermine your confidence or make you feel unworthy.

Practice Gratitude

Cultivating gratitude can shift your focus from what's lacking to what you have. Each day, take a moment to reflect on the things you're grateful for, whether it's your accomplishments, relationships, or personal qualities. Gratitude enhances your sense of abundance and reinforces your self-worth.

Engage in Activities You Love

Pursue activities and hobbies that bring you joy and fulfillment. Engaging in activities you love helps you stay connected to your true self and reinforces your sense of worth. Whether it's painting, dancing, hiking, or volunteering, make time for activities that nourish your soul.

The Impact of Confidence on Relationships

Confidence has a profound impact on your relationships. When you believe in yourself and recognize your worth, you attract partners who value and respect you. Confident individuals are more likely to set healthy boundaries, communicate effectively, and maintain a sense of autonomy within their relationships.

A confident partner is attractive because they bring positivity, strength, and assurance to the relationship. They are secure in themselves, which allows them to support and uplift their partner without feeling threatened or insecure. This dynamic creates a balanced and fulfilling partnership based on mutual respect and admiration.

Conversely, lack of confidence can lead to unhealthy relationship patterns, such as dependency, jealousy, and insecurity. When you rely on your partner for validation or self-worth, you may feel threatened by their independence or success. This can create tension and conflict within the relationship.

Building confidence allows you to approach relationships from a place of strength and security. You can engage in healthy, supportive partnerships where both individuals contribute to each other's growth and well-being. Confident individuals are also better equipped to handle conflicts and challenges within the relationship, as they trust their ability to navigate difficult situations.

Real-Life Scenarios

To illustrate the transformative power of confidence, let's consider some real-life scenarios:

The Career Transition

Rachel is considering a major career change but is plagued by self-doubt. She worries that she doesn't have the necessary skills or experience to succeed in her new field. By focusing on building her confidence, Rachel starts setting small, achievable goals related to her career transition. She takes online courses, networks with professionals in her desired field, and celebrates each milestone. Over time, Rachel's confidence grows, and she successfully transitions to her new career, attracting opportunities and recognition for her efforts.

The Relationship Renewal

David and Mia have been together for several years, but Mia's lack of confidence has created tension in their relationship. She often seeks validation from David and feels threatened by his independence. By working on her confidence, Mia starts setting boundaries, pursuing her interests, and practicing positive affirmations. As Mia's self-assurance grows, she becomes more secure in herself and her relationship. David notices the positive change and feels more connected and supportive. Their relationship is revitalized, with both partners feeling more balanced and fulfilled.

The Personal Triumph

Carlos has always struggled with self-worth due to past experiences and critical feedback from others. He decides to focus on cultivating his self-worth by practicing self-compassion, setting boundaries, and surrounding himself with positive influences. Carlos also engages in activities he loves, such as writing and hiking. As he embraces his intrinsic value, Carlos feels more confident and fulfilled. He forms healthier relationships, achieves personal goals, and experiences a profound sense of inner peace.

Confidence is a transformative force that can reshape every aspect of your life. By building self-assurance and cultivating self-worth, you unlock your true potential and create a life rich in meaning, purpose, and authentic connections. This chapter has explored the foundations of confidence, practical tips and exercises to build self-assurance, and the impact of confidence on your relationships.

As you continue your journey, remember that confidence is a skill that requires continuous effort and practice.

Embrace the process, celebrate your progress, and trust in your ability to navigate life's challenges with strength and resilience. By unleashing your confidence, you open the door to a world of possibilities, empowering yourself to live a life that is true to your values, passions, and dreams.

Chapter 3

Self-Discovery: Uncovering Your True Self and Values

In the journey of life, there is perhaps no pursuit more significant and transformative than the quest for self-discovery. Understanding who you truly are at your core, recognizing your values, identifying your passions, and acknowledging your desires can fundamentally change the way you interact with the world and with others. In relationships, this deep self-awareness not only enhances the connection you have with yourself but also attracts partners who appreciate and resonate with your authenticity.

The Importance of Self-Discovery

Self-discovery is about peeling away the layers of societal expectations, external validations, and superficial desires to uncover the essence of who you truly are. It involves introspection, reflection, and a willingness to confront both your strengths and weaknesses. Knowing yourself deeply enables you to make choices that align with your true self, fostering a life of authenticity and fulfillment.

In relationships, self-discovery plays a crucial role. When you understand your values and what you stand for, you are better equipped to communicate your needs and boundaries. You attract partners who appreciate and respect your true self, rather than a facade. This foundation of authenticity leads to deeper, more meaningful connections.

Uncovering Your Values

Values are the principles and beliefs that guide your behavior and decisions. They are the compass that directs your life's journey. Identifying and understanding your values is a critical aspect of self-discovery. Here are some steps to uncover your values:

Reflection and Introspection

Take time to reflect on moments in your life when you felt truly content and fulfilled. What were you doing? Who were you with? What values were being honored in those moments? Similarly, think about times when you felt unhappy or conflicted. What values were being compromised?

Identify Core Values

Make a list of values that resonate with you. These could include honesty, integrity, compassion, creativity, freedom, or growth. Once you have a list, narrow it down to your top five core values. These are the values that are most important to you and that you strive to uphold in your daily life.

Evaluate Alignment

Assess how well your current life aligns with your core values. Are you living in a way that honors these values? If not, what changes can you make to bring your life into greater alignment with your core values?

Communicate Your Values

Once you are clear on your values, communicate them openly in your relationships. Share your values with your partner and discuss how you can both support and honor each other's values. This open communication fosters mutual respect and understanding.

Discovering Your Passions

Passions are the activities, interests, and pursuits that ignite your enthusiasm and bring you joy. They are the things that make you feel alive and connected to your true self. Discovering your passions is an essential part of self-discovery. Here's how you can uncover your passions:

Explore and Experiment

Try new activities and experiences to discover what you enjoy. Take up a new hobby, join a club, or attend workshops and events. Be open to exploring different interests and see what resonates with you.

Reflect on Childhood Interests

Think back to your childhood and the activities that brought you joy. Often, our childhood interests can provide clues to our true passions. What did you love doing as a child? How can you incorporate those activities into your adult life?

Listen to Your Heart

Pay attention to the activities that make you lose track of time, the topics that you love to talk about, and the pursuits that fill you with excitement. These are often indicators of your passions. Trust your instincts and follow what feels right.

Align with Your Values

Ensure that your passions align with your core values. When your passions and values are in harmony, you experience a deeper sense of fulfillment and purpose.

Integrate Passions into Your Life

Make time for your passions in your daily life. Whether it's a career, a hobby, or a volunteer activity, integrating your passions into your routine brings joy and fulfillment. Share your passions with your partner and explore ways to support each other's interests.

Acknowledging Your Desires

Desires are the things you long for, the dreams you hold, and the goals you strive to achieve. Acknowledging your desires is a crucial step in self-discovery. Here's how you can recognize and honor your desires:

Dream Big

Allow yourself to dream without limitations. What do you truly want in life? What are your deepest desires and aspirations? Write them down and visualize yourself achieving them.

Set Goals

Once you are clear on your desires, set specific, achievable goals to help you work towards them. Break down your goals into smaller, manageable steps and create a plan of action.

Take Action

Taking consistent action towards your desires is essential. Even small steps can lead to significant progress over time. Stay committed to your goals and trust the process.

Overcome Obstacles

Recognize that obstacles and challenges are a part of the journey. Stay resilient and find ways to overcome setbacks. Seek support from friends, family, or a mentor when needed.

Celebrate Achievements

Celebrate your progress and achievements along the way. Acknowledging your accomplishments boosts your confidence and motivation to keep moving forward.

Enhancing Relationships Through Self-Discovery

Self-discovery has a profound impact on relationships. When you know yourself deeply, you bring authenticity, clarity, and confidence to your interactions with others. Here's how self-discovery enhances relationships:

Attracting Compatible Partners

When you are clear on your values, passions, and desires, you attract partners who resonate with your true self. Authenticity attracts authenticity, leading to more meaningful and fulfilling relationships.

Communicating Effectively

Self-awareness enhances your ability to communicate effectively. You can express your needs, boundaries, and desires with clarity and confidence. Open and honest communication fosters mutual understanding and strengthens the connection with your partner.

Building Trust and Respect

Being authentic and true to yourself builds trust and respect in relationships. When you honor your values and passions, you set a positive example for your partner and create a foundation of mutual respect.

Supporting Each Other's Growth

Self-discovery encourages personal growth and development. When both partners are committed to self-discovery, they can support and inspire each other's growth, leading to a dynamic and evolving relationship.

Enhancing Intimacy

Deep self-awareness enhances emotional and physical intimacy. When you are in tune with your true self, you can connect with your partner on a deeper level, fostering a more intimate and satisfying relationship.

Real-Life Scenarios

To illustrate the power of self-discovery, let's consider some real-life scenarios:

The Career Shift

Samantha has always felt unfulfilled in her corporate job. Through self-discovery, she realizes that her true passion lies in creative writing. She decides to pursue her passion by taking writing courses and dedicating time to her craft. As she aligns her career with her passion,

Samantha feels more fulfilled and content. Her newfound confidence and happiness positively impact her relationships, as she shares her journey and dreams with her partner.

The Relationship Renewal

Mark and Sarah have been together for several years, but their relationship has become stagnant. Through self-discovery, Sarah realizes that she has been neglecting her own needs and passions. She starts exploring her interests, setting boundaries, and pursuing activities that bring her joy. As Sarah becomes more authentic and true to herself, she re-energizes the relationship. Mark is inspired by her growth and they both commit to supporting each other's self-discovery journeys.

The Personal Triumph

Carlos has always struggled with self-worth due to past experiences and critical feedback from others. He decides to focus on cultivating his self-worth by practicing self-compassion, setting boundaries, and surrounding himself with positive influences. Carlos also engages in activities he loves, such as writing and hiking. As he embraces his intrinsic value, Carlos feels more confident and fulfilled. He forms healthier relationships, achieves personal goals, and experiences a profound sense of inner peace.

Exercises for Self-Discovery

To aid in your journey of self-discovery, here are some exercises that you can incorporate into your daily routine:

Journaling

Journaling is a powerful tool for self-reflection and self-awareness. Take time each day to write about your thoughts, feelings, and experiences. Reflect on what brings you joy, what challenges you, and what you aspire to achieve. Journaling helps you gain insights into your true self and track your progress.

Meditation

Meditation helps quiet the mind and connect with your inner self. Practice mindfulness meditation to stay present and observe your thoughts without judgment. Meditation enhances self-awareness and helps you uncover your true desires and values.

Self-Reflection

Set aside time for self-reflection. Ask yourself questions like, "What are my core values?" "What activities make me feel most alive?" and "What do I truly want in life?" Reflect on your answers and explore how you can align your life with your true self.

Vision Board

Create a vision board that represents your dreams, goals, and aspirations. Use images, quotes, and words that inspire you. Display the vision board in a place where you can see it daily. It serves as a visual reminder of your true self and the life you want to create.

Seek Feedback

Seek feedback from trusted friends, family, or mentors. Ask them to share their observations about your strengths, passions, and values. Sometimes, others can see aspects of yourself that you may not be aware of. Use their feedback to gain deeper insights into your true self.

Self-discovery is a transformative journey that empowers you to live authentically and build meaningful relationships. By uncovering your true self, values, passions, and desires, you enhance your connection with yourself and attract partners who appreciate your authenticity. Embrace the process of self-discovery with curiosity and openness. Trust in your ability to navigate this journey and celebrate the growth and fulfillment it brings.

As you continue your journey of self-discovery, remember that it is a continuous process. Stay committed to exploring and understanding yourself. Embrace your true self with love and compassion. By doing so, you create a life that is aligned with your values, passions, and dreams, and you build relationships that are rich in authenticity, respect, and love.

Chapter 4

Commanding Respect: Earning and Maintaining Respect in Relationships

Respect is the cornerstone of any healthy and fulfilling relationship. It is the bedrock upon which trust, love, and mutual understanding are built. Commanding and maintaining respect in relationships is not just about asserting your worth but also about fostering an environment where both partners feel valued, heard, and supported. It looks into the dynamics of respect in relationships, providing insights and strategies on how to command and maintain respect from men, thereby fostering healthy and balanced partnerships.

Understanding the Dynamics of Respect

Respect in relationships goes beyond simple politeness or courtesy. It encompasses recognizing and valuing each other's individuality, boundaries, and contributions.

Respect is about honoring the other person's thoughts, feelings, and experiences, even when they differ from your own. It involves active listening, empathy, and genuine appreciation for each other's unique qualities.

In the context of romantic relationships, respect is a mutual exchange. It is not something that can be demanded or forced; it must be earned and nurtured through consistent actions and behaviors. Here are the key dynamics of respect in relationships:

Mutual Recognition

Respect involves recognizing each other's individuality and autonomy. It means seeing your partner as an equal, with their own thoughts, feelings, and desires. Mutual recognition fosters a sense of equality and partnership in the relationship.

Boundaries

Respecting boundaries is crucial in maintaining a healthy relationship. Boundaries are the limits that define what is acceptable and unacceptable behavior. They protect your emotional and physical well-being. Respecting boundaries means honoring your partner's limits and expecting the same in return.

Communication

Open and honest communication is fundamental to respect. It involves actively listening to your partner, expressing your thoughts and feelings clearly, and resolving conflicts constructively. Communication fosters understanding and respect between partners.

Trust

Trust is built on a foundation of respect. When you respect your partner, you build trust by being reliable, honest, and supportive. Trust and respect reinforce each other, creating a strong bond in the relationship.

Empathy

Empathy is the ability to understand and share your partner's feelings. It involves putting yourself in their shoes and seeing things from their perspective. Empathy fosters a deeper connection and mutual respect.

Earning Respect

Earning respect in a relationship requires consistent effort and a commitment to personal growth and integrity. Here are some strategies to help you earn respect from your partner:

Self-Respect

Respect begins with self-respect. When you value and honor yourself, you set the standard for how others should treat you. Self-respect involves recognizing your worth, setting boundaries, and practicing self-care. When you respect yourself, others are more likely to respect you as well.

Assertiveness

Being assertive means expressing your needs, desires, and boundaries clearly and confidently. It involves standing up for yourself in a respectful and constructive manner. Assertiveness is different from aggression; it is about communicating your needs without disregarding the needs of others. Assertive communication fosters respect by showing that you value yourself and your partner.

Consistency

Consistency is key to earning respect. Your actions and words should align with your values and principles. Consistency builds trust and reliability, demonstrating that you are dependable and authentic.

Integrity

Integrity involves being honest, transparent, and ethical in your actions and decisions. It means doing the right thing, even when it's difficult. Integrity fosters respect by showing that you are trustworthy and principled.

Empathy and Understanding

Show empathy and understanding towards your partner's feelings and experiences. Listen actively and validate their emotions. Empathy demonstrates that you value and respect their perspective, fostering mutual respect.

Support and Encouragement

Support your partner's goals and aspirations. Encourage them to pursue their dreams and be their cheerleader. Offering support and encouragement shows that you respect their individuality and growth.

Maintaining Respect

Maintaining respect in a relationship requires ongoing effort and commitment. Here are some strategies to help you maintain respect:

Continuous Communication

Keep the lines of communication open. Regularly check in with your partner about their needs, feelings, and concerns. Address conflicts and misunderstandings promptly and constructively. Continuous communication fosters ongoing respect and understanding.

Mutual Appreciation

Show appreciation for your partner's contributions and efforts. Express gratitude for the little things they do.

Mutual appreciation reinforces respect and strengthens the bond between partners.

Reinforce Boundaries

Respect and reinforce each other's boundaries. Boundaries may evolve over time, so it's important to revisit and reaffirm them regularly. Reinforcing boundaries ensures that both partners feel safe and respected.

Practice Empathy

Continue to practice empathy and understanding. Be mindful of your partner's feelings and experiences. Empathy fosters a deeper connection and mutual respect.

Personal Growth

Commit to personal growth and self-improvement. Pursue your passions, develop new skills, and strive to be the best version of yourself. Personal growth inspires respect and admiration from your partner.

Conflict Resolution

Handle conflicts with respect and empathy. Avoid blame and criticism, and focus on finding solutions that honor both partners' needs. Constructive conflict resolution maintains respect and harmony in the relationship.

Real-Life Scenarios

To illustrate the principles of commanding and maintaining respect, let's consider some real-life scenarios:

Setting Boundaries

Emma and John have been in a relationship for a few years. Emma values her personal space and time for self-care, but John often intrudes on this time. Emma decides to have a candid conversation with John about her need for personal space. She explains how this time helps her recharge and be a better partner. John listens and agrees to respect Emma's boundaries. By setting and respecting boundaries, Emma and John maintain mutual respect and a healthy balance in their relationship.

Assertive Communication

Sarah feels overwhelmed with household responsibilities and needs more support from her partner, Mark. Instead of bottling up her feelings, Sarah decides to have an assertive conversation with Mark. She expresses her feelings calmly and clearly, explaining how the imbalance affects her well-being. Mark listens and agrees to take on more responsibilities. Sarah's assertive communication fosters respect and understanding, strengthening their partnership.

Continuous Growth

Michael and Lisa have been married for several years. They both value personal growth and support each other's aspirations. Michael decides to pursue a new career path, and Lisa encourages him wholeheartedly. She attends his workshops, helps him with research, and celebrates his achievements. Michael feels respected and supported, and their relationship grows stronger as they continue to inspire each other's growth.

Exercises for Commanding and Maintaining Respect

Here are some exercises to help you command and maintain respect in your relationship:

Reflect on Self-Respect

Take time to reflect on your self-worth and self-respect. Write down your core values and principles. Identify areas where you need to set boundaries or practice self-care. Commit to honoring your self-respect in your daily life.

Practice Assertive Communication

Identify a situation where you need to express your needs or boundaries. Plan how you will communicate assertively, using "I" statements and focusing on your feelings and needs. Practice the conversation with a friend or in front of a mirror. When you're ready, have the conversation with your partner.

Show Appreciation

Make it a habit to show appreciation for your partner's efforts and contributions. Write a list of things you appreciate about your partner and share it with them. Express gratitude regularly and genuinely.

Empathy Exercises

Practice empathy by putting yourself in your partner's shoes. When your partner shares their feelings, listen actively and validate their emotions. Reflect on how you can show more empathy and understanding in your relationship.

Set and Reinforce Boundaries

Identify areas where you need to set or reinforce boundaries. Have a conversation with your partner about your boundaries and why they are important. Revisit and reaffirm boundaries regularly to ensure mutual respect.

Respect is the foundation of a healthy and fulfilling relationship. Commanding and maintaining respect requires self-awareness, assertiveness, integrity, empathy, and continuous effort. By understanding the dynamics of respect and implementing the strategies outlined in this chapter, you can create a relationship where both partners feel valued, heard, and supported.

Remember, respect begins with self-respect. Honor your worth, set clear boundaries, and communicate assertively. Foster mutual appreciation and empathy, and commit to personal growth. By doing so, you not only command respect from your partner but also create a partnership built on trust, love, and mutual respect.

As you continue your journey, embrace the process of commanding and maintaining respect with dedication and compassion. Celebrate the growth and fulfillment that respect brings to your relationship, and trust in your ability to create a partnership that honors and uplifts both you and your partner.

Chapter 5

Celebrating Independence: The Beauty of Autonomy and Self-Sufficiency

Independence is not just a state of being; it is a profound expression of self-worth and personal strength. Celebrating independence is about recognizing and honoring the power that comes from being self-sufficient and autonomous. This focuses and looks into the beauty of autonomy, exploring how it empowers women and fosters healthier, more balanced relationships.

Independence is the cornerstone of a fulfilling life. It allows women to navigate their paths, make their decisions, and live according to their values. This autonomy is deeply empowering, providing a sense of control and self-respect that is crucial for personal growth. When women embrace their independence, they demonstrate to themselves and others that they are capable and confident, able to handle life's challenges with grace and resilience.

Self-sufficiency is closely linked to independence, as it involves relying on oneself for emotional and financial stability. Women who are self-sufficient do not depend on others for their happiness or sense of worth. Instead, they cultivate their strengths and capabilities, building a solid foundation for their lives. This self-reliance is not about rejecting support from others but about ensuring that one's sense of identity and well-being is not contingent on external validation.

In relationships, the beauty of autonomy shines brightly. Independent women bring a unique dynamic to their partnerships, characterized by mutual respect and equality. They enter relationships not out of need but out of choice, seeking companionship that complements their lives rather than completes them. This distinction is crucial, as it shifts the focus from dependency to interdependency, where both partners support and uplift each other while maintaining their individual identities.

Men who appreciate strong, independent women are drawn to their confidence and self-assuredness. These qualities are attractive because they reflect a deep sense of self-awareness and inner strength. An independent woman is not afraid to assert her needs and boundaries, fostering a relationship environment where open communication and respect thrive. This mutual respect is the bedrock of a healthy and fulfilling partnership, where both individuals feel valued and empowered.

The celebration of independence also involves acknowledging the journey to self-sufficiency. For many women, achieving independence is a path filled with challenges and triumphs. It requires overcoming societal expectations, breaking free from limiting beliefs, and embracing one's true potential. By celebrating this journey, women can inspire others to pursue their paths to autonomy and self-reliance, creating a ripple effect of empowerment and strength.

Moreover, independence fosters a sense of adventure and curiosity about life. Independent women are often driven by a desire to explore new opportunities, learn new skills, and continually grow. This zest for life enriches their relationships, bringing vitality and excitement to their partnerships. Men who value independent women appreciate this adventurous spirit, as it keeps the relationship dynamic and engaging.

It is essential to understand that celebrating independence does not mean rejecting intimacy or connection. Instead, it involves creating a balanced approach to relationships, where both partners can thrive individually and together. Independent women know how to nurture their connections without losing themselves in the process. They understand the importance of personal space and self-care, ensuring that they remain whole and healthy individuals within their relationships.

Financial independence is another critical aspect of self-sufficiency. Women who manage their finances effectively demonstrate responsibility and foresight. Financial independence provides a sense of security and freedom, allowing women to make choices that align with their values and goals. This financial stability is attractive to partners, as it signifies maturity and stability, essential components of a lasting relationship.

Emotional independence is equally important. Women who are emotionally self-sufficient can manage their feelings and cope with life's ups and downs without relying excessively on their partners. This emotional resilience creates a stable and supportive relationship environment, where both individuals can grow and flourish. Emotional independence does not mean suppressing emotions but rather understanding and processing them healthily and constructively.

The celebration of independence also involves embracing one's passions and interests. Independent women pursue their hobbies and dreams with enthusiasm, bringing a rich tapestry of experiences and perspectives to their relationships. This pursuit of passions not only fulfills them personally but also adds depth and richness to their partnerships. Men who value independent women are often inspired by their dedication and drive, finding motivation in their partner's commitment to their dreams.

Celebrating independence is about recognizing and honoring the beauty of autonomy and self-sufficiency. These qualities empower women, enabling them to lead fulfilling lives and create strong, healthy relationships. Independence fosters mutual respect, open communication, and emotional resilience, all crucial for a successful partnership. By embracing and celebrating their independence, women can inspire others to do the same, creating a world where autonomy and self-sufficiency are celebrated and valued.

Chapter 6

The Secrets of Attraction: Why Men Are Drawn to Strong Women

Attraction is a complex and multifaceted phenomenon, driven by a myriad of psychological, emotional, and social factors. Understanding why men are irresistibly drawn to strong, confident women requires delving into the principles of attraction and the dynamics that underlie successful relationships. We will explore the secrets of attraction and uncover why self-assured women hold a unique and compelling allure for men.

At the heart of attraction lies the concept of confidence. Confidence is universally appealing because it signifies self-assuredness, competence, and a strong sense of identity. Men are naturally drawn to women who exhibit confidence because it suggests that they know who they are and what they want from life. This self-assuredness is magnetic, creating an aura of intrigue and admiration.

Confident women project an inner strength that is both empowering and captivating, making them irresistible to those who seek partners who can stand independently and shine brightly.

Confidence also communicates a sense of security and stability. In the context of relationships, this is crucial because it provides a foundation of trust and reliability. Men find confident women attractive because they exude an air of dependability and resilience. They are perceived as partners who can handle life's challenges with grace and fortitude, making them ideal companions for a journey through life's ups and downs. This sense of security fosters a deep emotional connection, as men feel assured that they can rely on their partners in times of need.

Self-assured women are also known for their strong sense of boundaries. They understand the importance of maintaining their autonomy and are not afraid to assert their needs and desires. This clarity of boundaries is attractive because it demonstrates respect for oneself and others. Men appreciate women who can communicate their limits effectively, as it leads to healthier and more balanced relationships. The ability to set and maintain boundaries is a sign of emotional maturity and self-respect, qualities that are highly valued in a partner.

Moreover, strong women possess a unique blend of independence and interdependence. They are capable of thriving on their own but also understand the value of a supportive partnership. This balance is crucial in creating a dynamic and fulfilling relationship. Men are drawn to women who can stand on their own two feet yet are willing to share their lives with someone else. This combination of self-sufficiency and openness to connection is incredibly appealing, as it creates a partnership based on mutual respect and collaboration.

The psychology of attraction also highlights the importance of authenticity. Authenticity involves being true to oneself and living in alignment with one's values and beliefs. Strong women are often admired for their authenticity because they are unapologetically themselves. They do not conform to societal expectations or seek validation from others. Instead, they embrace their individuality and live their truth with confidence. This authenticity is captivating because it creates a sense of genuineness and trust. Men are attracted to women who are real and honest, as it fosters a deep emotional connection and intimacy.

Another key factor in attraction is emotional intelligence. Emotional intelligence involves the ability to understand and manage one's emotions and the emotions of others. Strong women often possess high emotional intelligence, allowing them to navigate relationships with empathy and understanding. This quality is attractive because it creates a nurturing and supportive environment within the relationship. Men appreciate partners who can communicate effectively, empathize with their experiences, and provide emotional support. Emotional intelligence enhances the depth and quality of the connection, making the relationship more fulfilling and meaningful.

The allure of strong women also lies in their passion and drive. They are often deeply committed to their goals and dreams, pursuing them with determination and enthusiasm. This passion is inspiring and attractive because it reflects a sense of purpose and ambition. Men are drawn to women who have a clear vision for their lives and are actively working towards their aspirations. This drive creates a dynamic and exciting partnership, as both individuals motivate and support each other in their endeavors.

Independence is another significant aspect of attraction. Independent women demonstrate that they do not need a partner to complete them but choose to share their lives with someone who complements them. This independence is attractive because it signifies a healthy and balanced approach to relationships. Men are drawn to women who can maintain their sense of self within a partnership, as it creates a relationship dynamic based on equality and mutual respect. Independent women bring a sense of strength and stability to the relationship, fostering a deep and lasting connection.

The physical aspect of attraction should not be overlooked. While emotional and psychological factors play a crucial role, physical attraction is also a significant component. Strong women often take care of their physical health and well-being, reflecting their overall confidence and self-respect. This attention to self-care is attractive because it signifies a holistic approach to life. Men are drawn to women who radiate vitality and energy, as it enhances the overall connection and intimacy within the relationship.

Furthermore, strong women possess a sense of adventure and curiosity about life. They are open to new experiences and are not afraid to step out of their comfort zones. This adventurous spirit is incredibly attractive because it brings excitement and spontaneity to the relationship. Men appreciate partners who are willing to explore new horizons and embrace life's opportunities with enthusiasm. This sense of adventure creates a dynamic and engaging partnership, where both individuals can grow and evolve together.

The beauty of attraction also lies in the sense of empowerment that strong women exude. Empowerment involves recognizing one's strengths and capabilities and using them to create a fulfilling and purposeful life. Men are irresistibly drawn to empowered women because they inspire and uplift those around them. This sense of empowerment creates a positive and supportive relationship environment, where both partners can thrive and achieve their fullest potential.

Lastly, the allure of strong women is deeply rooted in their ability to foster a sense of partnership and collaboration. They understand that successful relationships are built on mutual support, respect, and understanding. Men are drawn to women who can create a balanced and harmonious partnership, where both individuals contribute equally and support each other's growth. This collaborative approach to relationships enhances the overall quality of the connection, creating a fulfilling and lasting bond.

The secrets of attraction lie in the qualities that strong, confident women embody. Confidence, self-assuredness, authenticity, emotional intelligence, passion, independence, physical vitality, a sense of adventure, empowerment, and a collaborative spirit are all key factors that make these women irresistibly attractive. By embracing and celebrating these qualities, women can create deep and meaningful connections with their partners, fostering relationships that are fulfilling, supportive, and enduring.

Chapter 7

Navigating Relationship Dynamics: Understanding Male-Female Interactions

Understanding the dynamics of male-female interactions is crucial for building harmonious and fulfilling relationships. These dynamics are influenced by a myriad of factors, including biological differences, social conditioning, emotional needs, and communication styles. We will look into the complexities of how men and women interact, exploring key principles that can help foster understanding and connection in relationships.

At the heart of male-female interactions lies the concept of communication. Effective communication is the cornerstone of any successful relationship, yet men and women often have different communication styles. Men tend to be more direct and solution-oriented in their communication, while women often seek to express and explore their emotions. Understanding these differences can help partners navigate conversations more effectively, reducing misunderstandings and fostering deeper connection. For instance, when a woman shares her feelings, a man may feel compelled to offer solutions, while she might simply be seeking empathy and understanding. Recognizing this dynamic allows both partners to adjust their approaches, leading to more satisfying interactions.

Emotional needs also play a significant role in relationship dynamics. Men and women often have different emotional requirements, which can sometimes lead to conflict if not properly addressed. Women typically need to feel heard, valued, and understood, while men often seek respect, appreciation, and support. These needs are deeply rooted in our psychological makeup and can influence how we relate to each other. By acknowledging and addressing each other's emotional needs, partners can create a more nurturing and supportive relationship environment. This involves active listening, validating each other's feelings, and expressing appreciation and respect regularly.

Biological differences between men and women also impact relationship dynamics. Hormonal fluctuations, for instance, can affect mood and behavior, leading to varying emotional responses. Understanding these biological factors can help partners show empathy and patience during challenging times. For example, recognizing the impact of hormonal changes on a woman's mood can encourage a man to offer additional support and understanding during certain periods. Similarly, understanding how testosterone levels influence a man's behavior can help a woman approach interactions with greater empathy and patience.

Social conditioning and cultural expectations also shape male-female interactions. From a young age, men and women are often taught different roles and behaviors based on societal norms. These expectations can influence how they perceive themselves and each other, sometimes leading to misunderstandings and conflicts.

Challenging these stereotypes and embracing a more egalitarian approach to relationships can help partners build more balanced and respectful connections. This involves questioning traditional gender roles and fostering an environment where both partners feel free to express themselves authentically.

Conflict resolution is another critical aspect of navigating relationship dynamics. Disagreements and conflicts are inevitable in any relationship, but how partners handle them can make a significant difference in the health and longevity of the relationship. Men and women often have different approaches to conflict resolution, with men tending to prefer direct and immediate solutions, while women may seek to discuss and process their feelings more thoroughly. Understanding these differences can help partners find a middle ground, allowing for effective resolution without escalating tensions. This involves practicing patience, active listening, and compromise, ensuring that both partners feel heard and respected.

The dynamics of power and control also play a role in male-female interactions. In some relationships, one partner may exert more control or influence, leading to an imbalance that can create tension and resentment. Striving for equality and mutual respect is crucial for maintaining a healthy and fulfilling relationship. This involves recognizing and addressing any power imbalances, ensuring that both partners have an equal say in decision-making and that their contributions are valued and respected.

Intimacy and vulnerability are fundamental components of relationship dynamics. Men and women often express and experience intimacy differently, with women generally being more comfortable with emotional vulnerability and men sometimes finding it challenging to open up. Creating a safe and supportive environment where both partners feel comfortable expressing their emotions and vulnerabilities is essential for deepening intimacy. This involves fostering trust, showing empathy, and encouraging open and honest communication about each other's needs and desires.

The role of empathy and compassion in male-female interactions cannot be overstated. Empathy involves understanding and sharing the feelings of another person, while compassion involves a genuine desire to help and support them. These qualities are vital for building strong and lasting relationships, as they enable partners to connect on a deeper emotional level. By practicing empathy and compassion, partners can better understand each other's perspectives, leading to more harmonious and fulfilling interactions. This involves actively listening to each other, showing genuine concern for each other's well-being, and offering support and encouragement during difficult times.

Sexual dynamics also play a significant role in male-female interactions. Sexual intimacy is a vital component of most romantic relationships, and understanding each other's sexual needs and desires is crucial for maintaining a satisfying and fulfilling connection. Men and women often have different sexual preferences and expectations, which can sometimes lead to misunderstandings or conflicts. Open and honest communication about sexual needs, preferences, and boundaries can help partners navigate these dynamics more effectively, ensuring that both individuals feel satisfied and respected in their sexual relationship. This involves discussing sexual desires and boundaries openly, showing respect for each other's preferences, and being willing to explore new ways to enhance sexual intimacy.

Trust and loyalty are fundamental pillars of any successful relationship. Trust involves believing in the reliability and integrity of one's partner, while loyalty involves a commitment to the relationship and each other. Building and maintaining trust and loyalty require consistent effort and dedication from both partners. This involves being honest and transparent with each other, keeping promises and commitments, and showing unwavering support and dedication to the relationship. By fostering trust and loyalty, partners can create a strong and unbreakable bond that withstands the test of time.

Shared values and goals are also crucial for building harmonious and fulfilling relationships. When partners share similar values and goals, they are more likely to work together towards common objectives, creating a sense of unity and purpose. This involves discussing and aligning each other's values, beliefs, and aspirations, ensuring that both partners are on the same page and working towards the same future. By sharing values and goals, partners can build a strong foundation for their relationship, ensuring that they are both moving in the same direction and supporting each other's dreams and aspirations.

Support and encouragement are vital for nurturing and sustaining a healthy relationship. Men and women both need to feel supported and encouraged by their partners, especially during challenging times. This involves offering emotional, practical, and moral support, showing genuine concern for each other's well-being, and celebrating each other's successes and achievements. By providing consistent support and encouragement, partners can create a positive and nurturing relationship environment, where both individuals feel valued and appreciated.

Navigating relationship dynamics involves understanding the complexities of male-female interactions and fostering a deep sense of connection and understanding. By recognizing and addressing differences in communication styles, emotional needs, biological factors, social conditioning, conflict resolution, power dynamics, intimacy, empathy, sexual dynamics, trust, loyalty, shared values, and support, partners can build harmonious and fulfilling relationships. These principles are the foundation of successful relationships, enabling partners to connect on a deeper level, support each other's growth, and create a lasting and meaningful bond. By embracing and celebrating these dynamics, men and women can build relationships that are truly fulfilling, supportive, and enduring.

Chapter 8

Mastering Communication: Effective Dialogue in Relationships

Communication is the lifeblood of any successful relationship. It is the bridge that connects two individuals, allowing them to share their thoughts, feelings, and desires. Mastering the art of effective dialogue is crucial for fostering understanding, connection, and intimacy in relationships. This explores comprehensive strategies and principles that can help partners communicate more effectively, ensuring a deeper and more fulfilling connection.

The foundation of effective communication lies in active listening. Active listening goes beyond simply hearing words; it involves fully engaging with your partner and understanding their perspective. When you listen actively, you show your partner that their thoughts and feelings are valued. This practice involves making eye contact, nodding in acknowledgment, and providing verbal affirmations that you are attentive. By prioritizing active listening, partners can create an environment where both individuals feel heard and respected, fostering mutual understanding and empathy.

Another crucial aspect of effective communication is empathy. Empathy is the ability to understand and share the feelings of another person. It involves putting yourself in your partner's shoes and genuinely trying to grasp their emotional experience. Empathy fosters a deeper connection by allowing partners to support each other on an emotional level. When you respond to your partner with empathy, you validate their feelings and show that you care about their well-being. This validation strengthens the emotional bond and creates a sense of intimacy and trust.

Clear and concise expression of thoughts and feelings is also essential for effective communication. Often, misunderstandings arise from ambiguous or indirect communication. To avoid this, it is important to express yourself clearly and directly. Use "I" statements to convey your feelings and needs without placing blame on your partner. For example, instead of saying, "You never listen to me," you might say, "I feel unheard when I don't get a chance to express my thoughts." This approach reduces defensiveness and encourages open dialogue, making it easier to resolve conflicts and understand each other's perspectives.

Nonverbal communication plays a significant role in effective dialogue as well. Body language, facial expressions, and tone of voice can convey emotions and intentions that words alone may not capture. Being mindful of your nonverbal cues and interpreting your partner's can enhance communication. For example, maintaining eye contact shows interest and sincerity, while crossed arms might indicate defensiveness or discomfort. By paying attention to these nonverbal signals, partners can ensure that their communication is more aligned and authentic.

Another critical component of mastering communication is timing. Knowing when to discuss certain topics is crucial for productive dialogue. Bringing up sensitive issues during moments of stress or fatigue can lead to unproductive and heated conversations. Instead, choose a time when both partners are calm and can give their full attention to the discussion. This thoughtful approach helps ensure that conversations are more constructive and less likely to escalate into conflicts.

Patience and understanding are also vital in effective communication. Relationships often involve complex emotions and situations that require time to process. Being patient with your partner and allowing them the space to express themselves fully can lead to more meaningful and productive conversations. This patience demonstrates respect and compassion, showing your partner that you value their thoughts and feelings.

Conflict resolution is an integral part of communication in relationships. Conflicts are inevitable, but how they are handled can make or break a relationship. Effective conflict resolution involves staying calm, listening actively, and addressing the issue rather than attacking the person. Focus on finding a solution that satisfies both partners rather than trying to "win" the argument. Compromise and collaboration are key to resolving conflicts in a way that strengthens the relationship rather than damaging it.

The role of trust in communication cannot be overstated. Trust is the foundation upon which open and honest dialogue is built. When partners trust each other, they feel safe to share their deepest thoughts and feelings without fear of judgment or rejection. Building trust involves being reliable, keeping promises, and showing consistency in your actions. Trust is also about being vulnerable and allowing your partner to see your authentic self. This mutual trust creates a safe space for open communication and deepens the emotional connection.

Cultural and individual differences can also influence communication styles. Understanding and respecting these differences is essential for effective dialogue. Partners may come from different backgrounds with varying norms and expectations around communication. Being aware of these differences and approaching them with curiosity and openness can prevent misunderstandings and foster a more inclusive and respectful dialogue. This cultural sensitivity enriches the relationship by allowing partners to appreciate and learn from each other's unique perspectives.

The importance of feedback in communication should not be overlooked. Constructive feedback helps partners understand each other's needs and improve their communication skills. When giving feedback, focus on specific behaviors rather than making generalizations. Use a positive and supportive tone, and express your feedback in a way that encourages growth rather than causing defensiveness. Similarly, being open to receiving feedback and viewing it as an opportunity for growth can enhance the quality of communication in the relationship.

Another effective strategy for improving communication is practicing mindfulness. Mindfulness involves being fully present in the moment and aware of your thoughts and feelings without judgment. Applying mindfulness to communication means being fully present during conversations and truly focusing on your partner's words and emotions. This practice enhances the quality of dialogue by ensuring that both partners are fully engaged and attentive.

Setting aside regular time for meaningful conversations can also strengthen communication in relationships. Life can be busy, and it's easy for important conversations to be neglected. By intentionally scheduling time for in-depth discussions, partners can ensure that they stay connected and address any issues before they escalate. This dedicated time allows for uninterrupted dialogue, where both partners can express themselves freely and work through any challenges together.

The role of gratitude and appreciation in communication is also significant. Expressing gratitude for your partner and acknowledging their positive qualities and contributions can enhance the overall tone of communication. This practice fosters a positive and supportive environment, where both partners feel valued and appreciated. Regularly expressing appreciation can strengthen the emotional bond and create a more harmonious relationship.

Effective communication also involves being adaptable and flexible. Relationships are dynamic, and partners' needs and circumstances can change over time. Being willing to adapt your communication style to meet your partner's evolving needs is crucial for maintaining a strong connection. This flexibility shows that you are attentive to your partner's well-being and committed to nurturing the relationship.

Another important aspect of communication is addressing and managing emotions. Emotions can greatly influence how we communicate, and being aware of this can help partners navigate conversations more effectively. Learning to identify and articulate your emotions can prevent misunderstandings and promote clearer dialogue. Additionally, managing emotions during heated conversations is crucial for maintaining respect and preventing escalation. Techniques such as deep breathing, taking a pause, or agreeing to revisit the conversation later can help manage emotional intensity and ensure more productive discussions.

The role of humor in communication should not be underestimated. Humor can lighten the mood and make difficult conversations more manageable. Sharing laughter and playful moments can strengthen the bond between partners and create a more relaxed and open communication environment. However, it's important to use humor appropriately and ensure it does not undermine the seriousness of the conversation or come across as dismissive.

Lastly, understanding the power dynamics in communication is crucial. Power imbalances can affect how partners communicate and perceive each other. Being aware of these dynamics and striving for equality in communication can foster a more respectful and balanced relationship. This involves ensuring that both partners have an equal voice and that their opinions and feelings are valued equally.

Mastering communication is essential for building and maintaining successful relationships. Effective dialogue involves active listening, empathy, clear expression, nonverbal communication, timing, patience, conflict resolution, trust, cultural sensitivity, feedback, mindfulness, dedicated time, gratitude, adaptability, emotional management, humor, and awareness of power dynamics. By incorporating these strategies into your interactions, you can foster understanding, connection, and intimacy in your relationship. Communication is not just about exchanging words; it is about connecting on a deeper level and creating a strong and lasting bond with your partner. Through effective communication, partners can navigate challenges, celebrate successes, and build a relationship that is truly fulfilling and enriching.

Chapter 9

Setting Healthy Boundaries: Maintaining Personal Space and Limits

Setting healthy boundaries is a fundamental aspect of any relationship. Boundaries help individuals maintain their sense of self, protect their personal space, and ensure that their needs and values are respected. In the context of romantic relationships, healthy boundaries are crucial for fostering mutual respect, trust, and intimacy. This explores the importance of boundaries, offers guidance on how to establish and maintain them, and discusses the positive impact they can have on a relationship.

Understanding what boundaries are is the first step in setting them. Boundaries are the limits we set for ourselves in relationships that define what we are comfortable with and what we are not. They can be physical, emotional, mental, or even spiritual. Physical boundaries pertain to personal space and physical touch, emotional boundaries involve protecting our feelings and emotional energy, mental boundaries relate to our thoughts and opinions, and spiritual boundaries concern our beliefs and values. Recognizing these different types of boundaries helps us understand their importance and the role they play in our well-being.

The importance of boundaries cannot be overstated. They are essential for maintaining a healthy sense of identity and self-respect. Without boundaries, individuals can feel overwhelmed, resentful, and even lost in their relationships. Boundaries help us take care of ourselves by ensuring that our needs and preferences are acknowledged and respected. They allow us to preserve our individuality while still being connected to others. By setting clear boundaries, we communicate our limits and expectations, which can prevent misunderstandings and conflicts.

One of the primary benefits of healthy boundaries is that they foster mutual respect. When both partners in a relationship understand and respect each other's boundaries, it creates an environment of trust and safety. This mutual respect strengthens the emotional bond and enhances intimacy. It also ensures that both partners feel valued and appreciated, which is crucial for the overall health of the relationship. Respecting boundaries means acknowledging each other's autonomy and recognizing that each individual has the right to their own space and limits.

Boundaries also play a vital role in managing conflicts. In any relationship, conflicts are inevitable. However, when boundaries are clearly defined, it becomes easier to navigate disagreements without causing harm or resentment. Boundaries provide a framework for how to approach conflicts in a respectful and constructive manner. They help partners communicate their needs and feelings without crossing each other's limits. This approach leads to more effective conflict resolution and helps maintain the harmony and balance in the relationship.

Establishing boundaries starts with self-awareness. Understanding your own needs, values, and limits is crucial for setting boundaries that are meaningful and effective. Take time to reflect on what is important to you and what makes you feel comfortable and safe. This self-awareness will guide you in defining your boundaries and communicating them to your partner. It is also important to recognize that boundaries can change over time. As individuals grow and evolve, their needs and limits may shift. Regular self-reflection helps ensure that your boundaries remain relevant and supportive of your well-being.

Communicating boundaries effectively is essential for their success. Clear and honest communication is key to ensuring that your partner understands and respects your limits. Use "I" statements to express your boundaries in a way that focuses on your needs rather than blaming or criticizing your partner. For example, instead of saying, "You always invade my privacy," you could say, "I need some alone time to recharge and feel more balanced." This approach reduces defensiveness and fosters open and constructive dialogue. It is also important to be specific and direct about your boundaries to avoid misunderstandings.

Another crucial aspect of setting boundaries is consistency. Once you have communicated your boundaries, it is important to consistently enforce them. This consistency shows your partner that you are serious about your limits and that they need to be respected. It also helps build trust, as your partner knows what to expect and can rely on you to maintain your boundaries. However, consistency does not mean rigidity. Flexibility is also important in relationships, and there may be times when it is appropriate to adjust your boundaries. The key is to communicate any changes clearly and ensure that they are mutually agreed upon.

Respecting your partner's boundaries is equally important. Just as you have your own limits, your partner also has their own needs and preferences. Respecting their boundaries shows that you value and appreciate them as an individual. It also helps create a balanced and reciprocal relationship where both partners feel respected and supported. Pay attention to your partner's verbal and nonverbal cues, and be willing to adjust your behavior to honor their boundaries. This mutual respect is the foundation of a healthy and fulfilling relationship.

Boundaries are not just about saying no; they are also about saying yes to what supports your well-being. Setting boundaries allows you to prioritize self-care and ensure that your own needs are met. This self-care is essential for maintaining your mental and emotional health, which in turn supports the health of your relationship. When you take care of yourself, you are better able to show up for your partner and contribute to the relationship in a positive and meaningful way.

One common misconception about boundaries is that they create distance in a relationship. In reality, healthy boundaries enhance intimacy by creating a safe and respectful environment where both partners feel free to be themselves. Boundaries allow for a balance between individuality and togetherness, ensuring that both partners can maintain their sense of self while still being connected. This balance is crucial for a healthy and lasting relationship.

Boundaries also play a role in preventing burnout and resentment. Without boundaries, individuals may feel overwhelmed by the demands of the relationship, leading to burnout and resentment. By setting limits on what you can and cannot do, you protect yourself from overextending and ensure that you have the energy and resources to nurture the relationship. This approach also prevents resentment, as both partners are clear about their expectations and limits.

Another important aspect of boundaries is that they help maintain healthy relationships outside of the romantic partnership. Friendships, family relationships, and work interactions all require boundaries to ensure that they are supportive and respectful. Setting boundaries in these areas allows you to maintain a balanced and fulfilling life, where all your relationships contribute positively to your well-being.

In some cases, setting boundaries may involve difficult conversations or even conflict. It is important to approach these situations with empathy and understanding. Recognize that setting boundaries is not about rejecting or pushing away your partner; it is about taking care of yourself and ensuring that the relationship is healthy and sustainable. Approach these conversations with compassion and a willingness to listen and understand your partner's perspective. This empathy can help navigate difficult conversations and ensure that both partners feel heard and respected.

Boundaries also play a role in maintaining independence within a relationship. Independence is essential for a healthy relationship, as it allows both partners to grow and thrive as individuals. Boundaries support this independence by ensuring that each partner has the space and freedom to pursue their own interests and goals. This independence enriches the relationship, as both partners bring their unique experiences and perspectives to the partnership.

Trust is a critical component of boundaries. When partners trust each other to respect their boundaries, it creates a sense of safety and security in the relationship. This trust allows for greater openness and vulnerability, enhancing the emotional connection between partners. Building and maintaining this trust requires consistent and respectful communication about boundaries and a commitment to honoring each other's limits.

Boundaries are also essential for managing external influences on the relationship. Family, friends, and social expectations can all impact a relationship, and setting boundaries helps protect the partnership from undue external pressures. This involves communicating with others about what is and is not acceptable in terms of their involvement in your relationship. It also means supporting your partner in setting their own boundaries with external influences. By protecting the relationship from external pressures, partners can focus on nurturing their connection and maintaining a healthy and balanced partnership.

One of the challenges of setting boundaries is dealing with guilt and fear. It is common to feel guilty about setting limits, especially if it means disappointing others. However, it is important to recognize that taking care of yourself is not selfish; it is essential for your well-being and the health of your relationship. Overcoming this guilt involves shifting your mindset to see boundaries as a form of self-respect and self-care. It is also important to address any fears you may have about setting boundaries, such as the fear of rejection or conflict. Recognizing and confronting these fears can help you feel more confident and empowered in setting and maintaining boundaries.

Setting healthy boundaries is essential for maintaining personal space and limits in a relationship. Boundaries help individuals maintain their sense of self, protect their well-being, and ensure that their needs and values are respected. They foster mutual respect, trust, and intimacy, and play a crucial role in conflict resolution and maintaining harmony in the relationship. By understanding the importance of boundaries, reflecting on your own needs and limits, communicating effectively, and respecting your partner's boundaries, you can create a balanced and fulfilling relationship. Boundaries are not about creating distance; they are about creating a safe and respectful environment where both partners can thrive as individuals and as a couple. Embracing boundaries as a form of self-care and self-respect allows you to prioritize your well-being and contribute positively to the relationship. Through healthy boundaries, partners can navigate challenges, prevent burnout and resentment, and maintain independence, ensuring a strong and lasting connection. Trust, empathy, and consistent communication are key to setting and maintaining boundaries, fostering a relationship built on mutual respect and support. By overcoming guilt and fear, and recognizing the positive impact of boundaries, individuals can create a relationship that is healthy, balanced, and deeply fulfilling.

Chapter 10

Nurturing Romance: Building and Sustaining Romantic Chemistry

Romance is often seen as the magical spark that ignites passion and connection in relationships. It is the ingredient that transforms a relationship from mere companionship to a deep, emotional bond filled with love and intimacy. Nurturing romance is not just about grand gestures or fleeting moments of excitement; it is about consistently building and sustaining romantic chemistry with your partner. It looks into the art of nurturing romance, exploring the ways to build strong, passionate connections and keep the romantic flame alive.

Understanding Romantic Chemistry

Romantic chemistry is that indescribable connection that makes your heart race and your spirits lift when you're with your partner. It encompasses physical attraction, emotional intimacy, and a deep sense of compatibility. While some believe that chemistry is something that just happens naturally, it can also be cultivated and enhanced through intentional actions and behaviors. Understanding what drives romantic chemistry in your relationship is the first step in nurturing it.

Physical attraction is often the initial spark that brings people together, but sustaining a romantic connection goes beyond the physical. Emotional intimacy plays a crucial role in deepening the romantic bond. This intimacy involves sharing your innermost thoughts, feelings, and experiences with your partner. It creates a sense of vulnerability and trust, allowing both partners to feel connected on a deeper level. Compatibility, which includes shared values, interests, and goals, also strengthens romantic chemistry by providing a foundation of mutual understanding and respect.

The Power of Small Gestures

In the pursuit of nurturing romance, small gestures often carry more weight than grand declarations of love. Simple acts of kindness and thoughtfulness can make a significant difference in maintaining a romantic connection. These gestures show your partner that you care about their happiness and well-being. They can be as simple as leaving a love note, surprising them with their favorite treat, or doing something special for them without being asked. These small acts of love and consideration can create a sense of appreciation and affection that strengthens the romantic bond.

Consistency is key when it comes to small gestures. Regularly expressing your love and appreciation through these acts keeps the romance alive and prevents it from becoming stagnant. It's important to understand and cater to your partner's love language, whether it's words of affirmation, acts of service, receiving gifts, quality time, or physical touch. By consistently speaking your partner's love language, you reinforce the romantic connection and ensure that they feel valued and cherished.

Creating Shared Experiences

Shared experiences are another powerful way to nurture romantic chemistry. Engaging in activities that you both enjoy creates opportunities for bonding and creating lasting memories. These experiences can range from adventurous trips and hobbies to simple pleasures like cooking together or taking a walk. The key is to find activities that bring joy and excitement to both partners, allowing them to connect on a deeper level.

Trying new things together can also invigorate the relationship and introduce an element of novelty. Exploring new interests, visiting new places, or learning something new as a couple can rekindle the excitement and curiosity that often accompanies the early stages of a relationship. These shared experiences create a sense of unity and teamwork, reinforcing the bond between partners.

Communication: The Heart of Romance

Effective communication is at the heart of any romantic relationship. Open and honest communication fosters emotional intimacy and helps partners understand each other's needs and desires. Discussing your feelings, hopes, and dreams with your partner creates a deeper connection and allows both partners to feel seen and heard. It is essential to communicate not just about the big things, but also about the small, everyday details that make up your lives.

Expressing love and appreciation verbally is a powerful way to nurture romance. Compliment your partner, express gratitude for their actions, and let them know how much they mean to you. Verbal affirmations of love and appreciation can create a positive and loving atmosphere in the relationship. Additionally, discussing and planning for your future together reinforces the sense of commitment and shared goals, which are crucial for sustaining a romantic connection.

Listening is equally important in communication. Being a good listener means paying attention to your partner's words, empathizing with their feelings, and responding thoughtfully. Active listening shows that you value their perspective and are invested in their well-being. This mutual exchange of thoughts and feelings fosters a deeper emotional connection and enhances the romantic chemistry between partners.

Physical Affection and Intimacy

Physical affection and intimacy are vital components of romantic chemistry. Physical touch, such as holding hands, hugging, kissing, and cuddling, creates a sense of closeness and comfort. These gestures of physical affection release oxytocin, the "love hormone," which promotes bonding and a sense of security in the relationship. Regular physical affection helps maintain the romantic connection and ensures that both partners feel loved and cherished.

Intimacy goes beyond physical touch and includes emotional and sexual intimacy. Emotional intimacy involves sharing your innermost thoughts and feelings, creating a safe space for vulnerability and trust. Sexual intimacy is an important aspect of romantic relationships, and maintaining a healthy and satisfying sexual connection can strengthen the romantic bond. It's essential to communicate openly about your needs and desires and to approach intimacy with a sense of mutual respect and consideration.

The Role of Surprise and Spontaneity

Surprise and spontaneity can infuse excitement and novelty into a relationship, keeping the romance alive. Surprising your partner with unexpected gestures or spontaneous adventures can create moments of joy and delight. These surprises don't have to be elaborate; they can be as simple as planning a surprise date night, leaving a sweet message, or arranging a spontaneous weekend getaway. The element of surprise adds an element of excitement and keeps the relationship dynamic and engaging.

However, it's important to balance surprise and spontaneity with predictability and stability. While surprises can enhance romance, a relationship also needs a foundation of reliability and consistency. Finding the right balance between spontaneity and stability ensures that the relationship remains both exciting and secure.

Quality Time Together

Quality time is a crucial ingredient in nurturing romance. Spending dedicated, uninterrupted time together allows partners to connect deeply and strengthen their bond. This time can be spent engaging in activities you both enjoy, having meaningful conversations, or simply being present with each other. The key is to focus on each other and prioritize your relationship during this time.

In today's fast-paced world, it's easy to get caught up in daily responsibilities and distractions. Making a conscious effort to set aside quality time for your partner demonstrates your commitment and appreciation for the relationship. Whether it's a weekly date night, a daily check-in, or a yearly vacation, prioritizing quality time helps maintain the romantic connection and ensures that both partners feel valued and loved.

Maintaining Individuality

While spending quality time together is important, maintaining individuality is equally crucial for nurturing romance. A healthy relationship involves two individuals who are confident and fulfilled in their own right. Pursuing your own interests, goals, and hobbies allows you to bring new experiences and perspectives into the relationship. This individuality enriches the partnership and prevents it from becoming codependent or stagnant.

Encouraging your partner to pursue their passions and supporting their individual growth fosters mutual respect and admiration. It also allows both partners to maintain a sense of autonomy and self-worth, which is essential for a balanced and fulfilling relationship. By nurturing your individuality, you contribute to a dynamic and vibrant romantic connection.

The Importance of Trust and Honesty

Trust and honesty are the cornerstones of any romantic relationship. Without trust, it is difficult to build and sustain a deep and meaningful connection. Trust involves being reliable, keeping promises, and demonstrating integrity in your actions. It means being honest and transparent with your partner, even when it's difficult. Building trust takes time and consistency, but it is essential for maintaining a strong and healthy relationship.

Honesty involves being open and truthful about your thoughts, feelings, and intentions. It means communicating openly about your needs and desires and being willing to address issues and conflicts honestly. Honesty fosters a sense of security and confidence in the relationship, allowing both partners to feel safe and valued. By cultivating trust and honesty, you create a solid foundation for romance to flourish.

Celebrating Milestones and Achievements

Celebrating milestones and achievements together strengthens the romantic bond and creates lasting memories. Whether it's anniversaries, birthdays, or personal accomplishments, taking the time to acknowledge and celebrate these moments shows your partner that you appreciate and value them. These celebrations provide an opportunity to reflect on your journey together and to express gratitude for your relationship.

Creating rituals and traditions around these celebrations can enhance their significance and create a sense of continuity and shared history. Whether it's a special date night, a meaningful gift, or a heartfelt message, these rituals reinforce the romantic connection and provide a sense of joy and fulfillment.

Handling Challenges with Grace

Every relationship faces challenges, and how partners navigate these challenges can significantly impact their romantic connection. Handling difficulties with grace and resilience involves approaching conflicts with empathy, patience, and a willingness to find solutions together. It means supporting each other through tough times and maintaining a sense of unity and teamwork.

When faced with challenges, it's important to communicate openly and honestly about your feelings and concerns. Approach conflicts with a problem-solving mindset rather than placing blame. Seek to understand your partner's perspective and work together to find compromises and solutions that benefit both partners. By handling challenges with grace, you strengthen your relationship and demonstrate your commitment to nurturing romance even in difficult times.

Practicing Gratitude

Gratitude is a powerful tool for nurturing romance. Regularly expressing gratitude for your partner and your relationship creates a positive and loving atmosphere. It involves acknowledging the small and big things your partner does and expressing appreciation for their presence in your life. Practicing gratitude fosters a sense of joy and contentment and reinforces the romantic connection.

Gratitude can be expressed in various ways, such as verbal affirmations, written notes, or acts of kindness. By making gratitude a regular practice, you create a culture of appreciation and love in your relationship. This positive focus enhances the romantic chemistry and ensures that both partners feel valued and cherished.

Emotional Vulnerability

Emotional vulnerability is a key component of deepening romantic chemistry. It involves being open and honest about your feelings, fears, and desires. Sharing your vulnerabilities creates a sense of intimacy and trust, allowing both partners to feel connected on a deeper level. It means letting your guard down and allowing your partner to see your true self.

Being emotionally vulnerable requires courage and trust in your partner. It involves taking the risk of being seen and understood. When both partners are willing to be vulnerable, it creates a safe space for emotional intimacy and strengthens the romantic bond. This vulnerability fosters a sense of closeness and connection that is essential for nurturing romance.

Consistent Effort and Commitment

Nurturing romance requires consistent effort and commitment. It's not something that happens automatically or by chance; it requires intentional actions and behaviors. This commitment involves prioritizing your relationship, making time for each other, and consistently expressing love and appreciation. It means being willing to put in the effort to keep the romantic flame alive, even when life gets busy or challenging.

Consistency in nurturing romance builds a sense of reliability and security in the relationship. It shows your partner that you are invested in their happiness and well-being. By making a consistent effort, you create a strong and lasting romantic connection that can withstand the tests of time.

Nurturing romance is an ongoing process that involves understanding and cultivating romantic chemistry, expressing love through small gestures, creating shared experiences, and maintaining effective communication. It requires physical affection, spontaneity, quality time, and maintaining individuality. Trust, honesty, celebrating milestones, handling challenges, practicing gratitude, and emotional vulnerability are all essential components of nurturing romance. Most importantly, it requires consistent effort and commitment to keep the romantic flame alive. By embracing these principles, partners can build and sustain strong, passionate connections that bring joy, fulfillment, and lasting love to their relationship.

Chapter 11

Personal Growth: Developing Your Passions and Interests

Personal growth is a lifelong journey that plays a pivotal role in enhancing both your individuality and your relationships. It involves continuously pursuing your passions and interests, expanding your knowledge and skills, and striving to become the best version of yourself. It looks into the significance of personal growth, exploring how developing your passions and interests can lead to a more fulfilling life and a more enriching partnership.

The Importance of Personal Growth

Personal growth is the process of self-improvement and self-discovery. It encompasses various aspects of life, including emotional, intellectual, physical, and spiritual development. Engaging in personal growth allows you to gain a deeper understanding of yourself, build self-confidence, and enhance your overall well-being. It is through this journey that you uncover your true potential and find greater satisfaction and fulfillment in life.

In the context of relationships, personal growth is equally vital. A healthy relationship is built on the foundation of two individuals who are confident, fulfilled, and continually evolving. When both partners are committed to their personal growth, they bring fresh perspectives, new experiences, and renewed energy into the relationship. This dynamic contributes to a more vibrant, balanced, and supportive partnership.

Passions are the activities, interests, and pursuits that ignite your enthusiasm and bring you joy. They are the things that you are naturally drawn to and that provide a sense of purpose and fulfillment. Pursuing your passions is a crucial aspect of personal growth, as it allows you to tap into your inner desires and explore what truly makes you happy.

To identify your passions, take some time to reflect on the activities that excite you and make you feel alive. Think about the hobbies you enjoy, the topics that intrigue you, and the skills you are eager to develop. Once you have identified your passions, make a conscious effort to integrate them into your daily life. Whether it's dedicating time to a creative hobby, learning a new language, or participating in a sport, engaging in your passions allows you to experience joy and fulfillment on a deeper level.

Pursuing your passions also provides an opportunity for self-expression and creativity. It allows you to channel your energy into something meaningful and to showcase your unique talents and abilities. This self-expression is an essential component of personal growth, as it helps you to develop a stronger sense of identity and to connect with your authentic self.

In addition to pursuing your passions, expanding your interests is another key aspect of personal growth. This involves stepping out of your comfort zone and exploring new activities, topics, and experiences. By broadening your horizons, you open yourself up to new possibilities and opportunities for growth.

Expanding your interests can take many forms, such as trying out a new hobby, attending workshops or classes, traveling to new destinations, or reading books on diverse subjects. The goal is to continually challenge yourself and to remain curious and open-minded. This willingness to explore new interests keeps your life dynamic and exciting and prevents you from becoming stagnant or complacent.

Moreover, expanding your interests can lead to the discovery of new passions and talents. It allows you to uncover hidden potential and to develop skills that you may not have known you possessed. This ongoing exploration and learning contribute to your personal growth and enhance your overall quality of life.

Balancing Individuality and Partnership

While personal growth is essential for individual fulfillment, it also plays a significant role in the context of a relationship. A healthy relationship involves a balance between individuality and partnership. It requires both partners to support each other's personal growth while also nurturing their connection as a couple.

Maintaining this balance involves encouraging and respecting each other's interests and passions. It means giving each other the space and freedom to pursue personal goals and aspirations. By supporting your partner's personal growth, you demonstrate your love and respect for their individuality and their journey of self-discovery.

At the same time, it's important to find ways to integrate your personal growth into your relationship. Share your passions and interests with your partner, and explore opportunities for joint activities and experiences. This integration allows both partners to benefit from each other's growth and to strengthen their bond through shared pursuits.

Setting personal goals is a powerful way to drive your personal growth and to stay focused on your aspirations. Goals provide a sense of direction and purpose, motivating you to take action and to achieve your desired outcomes. They also help you to measure your progress and to stay committed to your growth journey.

When setting personal goals, it's important to be specific and realistic. Identify what you want to achieve, and break down your goals into manageable steps. Create a timeline for achieving your goals, and establish a plan of action. This structured approach increases your chances of success and keeps you motivated and accountable.

In the context of a relationship, sharing your personal goals with your partner can enhance your mutual support and understanding. Discussing your goals allows your partner to understand your aspirations and to offer encouragement and assistance. It also provides an opportunity for collaboration, as you can work together to achieve common goals and to support each other's individual pursuits.

Lifelong learning is a fundamental aspect of personal growth. It involves continuously seeking knowledge, developing new skills, and expanding your understanding of the world. Embracing lifelong learning keeps your mind active and engaged, and it fosters a sense of curiosity and intellectual fulfillment.

There are numerous ways to engage in lifelong learning, such as enrolling in educational courses, attending seminars and workshops, reading books and articles, or engaging in online learning platforms. The key is to remain open to new information and to actively seek opportunities for learning and development.

Lifelong learning also enhances your adaptability and resilience, enabling you to navigate life's challenges with greater confidence and resourcefulness. It equips you with the knowledge and skills needed to thrive in an ever-changing world, and it contributes to your overall sense of personal and professional fulfillment.

Building Resilience and Emotional Intelligence

Resilience and emotional intelligence are critical components of personal growth. Resilience is the ability to bounce back from adversity and to navigate challenges with strength and determination. Emotional intelligence involves understanding and managing your emotions, as well as recognizing and empathizing with the emotions of others.

Building resilience involves developing a positive mindset, cultivating coping strategies, and seeking support when needed. It requires a willingness to embrace challenges as opportunities for growth and to learn from setbacks. Resilience allows you to persevere in the face of difficulties and to emerge stronger and more capable.

Emotional intelligence, on the other hand, enhances your ability to communicate effectively, build meaningful relationships, and navigate social interactions with empathy and understanding. It involves self-awareness, self-regulation, empathy, and social skills. By developing emotional intelligence, you improve your interpersonal relationships and create a more harmonious and supportive environment in both your personal and professional life.

Mindfulness and self-reflection are powerful practices for personal growth. Mindfulness involves being present in the moment and fully engaging with your experiences. It allows you to develop a deeper awareness of your thoughts, emotions, and surroundings, and to respond to situations with greater clarity and intention.

Practicing mindfulness can take many forms, such as meditation, deep breathing exercises, or simply paying attention to your daily activities with a sense of presence and curiosity. By cultivating mindfulness, you enhance your ability to manage stress, improve your focus and concentration, and foster a greater sense of inner peace and well-being.

Self-reflection, on the other hand, involves taking the time to reflect on your experiences, thoughts, and behaviors. It allows you to gain insight into your strengths and areas for improvement, and to identify patterns and habits that may be holding you back. Self-reflection is a powerful tool for self-discovery and personal growth, as it provides the opportunity for continuous learning and self-improvement.

Seeking Mentorship and Guidance

Seeking mentorship and guidance is an effective way to support your personal growth journey. A mentor is someone who provides advice, support, and encouragement, and who can offer valuable insights based on their own experiences and expertise. Mentorship can take many forms, such as formal mentoring programs, coaching relationships, or informal guidance from trusted individuals.

A mentor can help you to identify your goals, navigate challenges, and stay motivated and focused on your growth journey. They can provide valuable feedback and perspective, and offer practical advice and strategies for achieving your aspirations. By seeking mentorship and guidance, you gain access to a wealth of knowledge and experience that can accelerate your personal growth and development.

Embracing change and adaptability is a crucial aspect of personal growth. Life is constantly evolving, and the ability to adapt to new circumstances and challenges is essential for personal and professional success. Embracing change involves being open to new experiences, being willing to take risks, and maintaining a flexible and resilient mindset.

Adaptability allows you to navigate uncertainty with confidence and to seize opportunities for growth and development. It involves a willingness to let go of old patterns and beliefs, and to embrace new ways of thinking and being. By cultivating adaptability, you enhance your ability to thrive in an ever-changing world and to continue growing and evolving throughout your life.

Physical well-being is an integral part of personal growth. Taking care of your physical health allows you to have the energy, vitality, and resilience needed to pursue your passions and interests. It involves maintaining a balanced diet, engaging in regular physical activity, getting adequate sleep, and managing stress.

Physical well-being also includes paying attention to your body's needs and seeking medical care when necessary. By prioritizing your physical health, you enhance your overall quality of life and ensure that you have the strength and stamina to achieve your personal and professional goals.

Building Strong Support Network

Building strong support networks is essential for personal growth. Surrounding yourself with supportive and like-minded individuals provides a sense of community and belonging, and offers valuable encouragement and motivation. These networks can include family members who understand your background and values, friends who share your interests, colleagues who inspire your professional aspirations, mentors who provide guidance and wisdom, and even online communities where you find like-minded individuals across the globe.

Support networks play a crucial role in personal growth by offering different perspectives, constructive feedback, and emotional support during both challenging times and moments of triumph. They serve as a safety net, providing reassurance and helping you stay resilient in the face of obstacles. By nurturing these relationships, you create a foundation of trust and mutual respect that fosters personal development and enriches your life.

Family members often provide unconditional love and support, serving as a constant source of encouragement throughout your journey of personal growth. They offer a deep understanding of your background and values, and their support can be invaluable in navigating life's challenges.

Friends who share your interests and values can provide companionship, laughter, and a sense of belonging. They offer encouragement and celebrate your achievements, while also offering a different perspective and constructive feedback when needed.

Colleagues and professional mentors play a vital role in your professional growth by providing guidance, advice, and opportunities for advancement. They offer insights into your industry or field of interest, help you navigate career transitions, and challenge you to expand your skills and knowledge.

Mentors, whether formal or informal, offer wisdom, experience, and perspective gained from their own journeys. They provide advice, encouragement, and support, helping you navigate challenges and make informed decisions. Their guidance can be invaluable in shaping your personal and professional development.

Online communities and networks connect you with like-minded individuals across the globe, offering support, inspiration, and opportunities for learning and growth. These communities provide a platform for sharing experiences, exchanging ideas, and expanding your horizons.

Building and nurturing strong support networks involves investing time and effort in cultivating meaningful relationships. It requires active listening, empathy, and reciprocity, as well as a willingness to offer support and encouragement to others in return. By surrounding yourself with supportive individuals who believe in your potential and share your values, you create a supportive environment that fosters personal growth, resilience, and fulfillment in all aspects of your life.

Chapter 12

The Journey to Self-Love: Fostering Self-Acceptance and Care

Self-love is the cornerstone of all healthy relationships. It is the deep-seated belief in your inherent worth and the commitment to treating yourself with kindness, respect, and compassion. Cultivating self-love and self-acceptance empowers you to bring your best self into your relationships, fostering deeper connections, and nurturing a more fulfilling life. It looks into the importance of self-love, exploring various ways to foster self-acceptance and care.

Understanding Self-Love

Self-love is often misunderstood as selfishness or narcissism, but it is far from that. True self-love involves recognizing your value, embracing your flaws and imperfections, and prioritizing your well-being. It is about treating yourself with the same kindness and compassion you would offer to a loved one. Self-love provides the foundation for emotional resilience, mental clarity, and a positive self-image.

At its core, self-love is about acceptance. It means accepting yourself as you are, without judgment or criticism. This acceptance includes acknowledging your strengths and achievements, as well as your weaknesses and mistakes. By embracing all aspects of yourself, you create a sense of inner peace and contentment that radiates into all areas of your life.

Self-acceptance is a crucial component of self-love. It involves recognizing and embracing your unique qualities, traits, and experiences. Self-acceptance means letting go of the need for external validation and approval, and instead finding validation within yourself. It is about being comfortable in your own skin and trusting in your worth.

Self-acceptance fosters a sense of authenticity and integrity. When you accept yourself fully, you are more likely to live in alignment with your true values and beliefs. This authenticity strengthens your relationships, as it allows you to show up as your true self and to connect with others on a deeper level.

Practices for Cultivating Self-Love

Positive Affirmations

Positive affirmations are powerful tools for fostering self-love and self-acceptance. They involve repeating positive statements about yourself to reinforce a healthy self-image. For example, you might say, "I am worthy of love and respect," or "I embrace my strengths and weaknesses." By consistently practicing positive affirmations, you can rewire your mindset and cultivate a more loving and accepting relationship with yourself.

Mindfulness and Meditation

Mindfulness and meditation practices help you to cultivate a sense of presence and self-awareness. These practices involve paying attention to your thoughts, emotions, and sensations without judgment. By practicing mindfulness, you can develop a deeper understanding of yourself and foster greater self-acceptance. Meditation can also help to calm the mind, reduce stress, and enhance your overall well-being.

Self-Compassion

Self-compassion involves treating yourself with kindness and understanding, especially during times of struggle or failure. It means offering yourself the same empathy and support you would extend to a friend. Self-compassion allows you to navigate challenges with greater resilience and to cultivate a more loving and forgiving relationship with yourself.

Setting Boundaries

Setting healthy boundaries is an essential aspect of self-love. Boundaries protect your well-being and ensure that you are not overextending yourself or compromising your values. Setting boundaries involves saying no when necessary, prioritizing your needs, and advocating for yourself. By setting and maintaining boundaries, you demonstrate self-respect and self-care.

Engaging in Self-Care

Self-care is a vital practice for nurturing self-love. It involves taking deliberate actions to care for your physical, emotional, and mental well-being. Self-care can include activities such as exercise, healthy eating, adequate sleep, relaxation, and engaging in hobbies and interests. By prioritizing self-care, you show yourself love and commitment to your overall well-being.

Overcoming Barriers to Self-Love

While self-love is essential, it can be challenging to cultivate, especially if you have experienced negative self-beliefs or external criticism. Overcoming barriers to self-love involves addressing these challenges and developing strategies to foster a more loving relationship with yourself.

Challenging Negative Self-Talk

Negative self-talk is a common barrier to self-love. It involves the critical and judgmental thoughts you have about yourself. To overcome this barrier, practice challenging and reframing negative self-talk. Replace self-criticism with positive and affirming statements. For example, instead of saying, "I'm not good enough," say, "I am capable and deserving of love and success."

Healing Past Wounds

Past experiences of trauma, rejection, or criticism can impact your ability to love yourself. Healing these wounds involves acknowledging and processing these experiences. This might include seeking therapy or counseling, engaging in self-reflection, or practicing forgiveness. By addressing past wounds, you can release the negative emotions and beliefs that hold you back from self-love.

Letting Go of Perfectionism

Perfectionism is the belief that you must be flawless to be worthy of love and acceptance. This unrealistic standard can hinder self-love and create a constant sense of inadequacy. Letting go of perfectionism involves embracing your imperfections and recognizing that you are worthy just as you are. It means valuing progress over perfection and celebrating your efforts and achievements.

Building Self-Esteem

Self-esteem is the sense of confidence and worthiness you have in yourself. Building self-esteem involves recognizing your strengths, accomplishments, and value. Practice self-affirmation, set achievable goals, and celebrate your successes. By building self-esteem, you reinforce a positive self-image and foster greater self-love.

The Role of Self-Love in Relationships

Self-love is the foundation of healthy and fulfilling relationships. When you love and accept yourself, you are better able to love and accept others. Self-love allows you to set healthy boundaries, communicate effectively, and navigate conflicts with compassion and understanding. It also enables you to show up authentically in your relationships, fostering deeper connections and mutual respect.

Healthy Boundaries

Self-love empowers you to set and maintain healthy boundaries in your relationships. Boundaries protect your well-being and ensure that your needs and values are respected. By setting boundaries, you create a balanced and respectful dynamic in your relationships.

Effective Communication

When you love and accept yourself, you are more likely to communicate openly and honestly. Self-love fosters self-awareness and confidence, allowing you to express your thoughts and feelings effectively. This open communication enhances understanding and connection in your relationships.

Conflict Resolution

Self-love enables you to navigate conflicts with compassion and understanding. It allows you to approach conflicts with a sense of empathy and a desire for resolution, rather than defensiveness or blame. By practicing self-love, you create a more harmonious and supportive relationship dynamic.

Mutual Respect

Self-love fosters a sense of mutual respect in your relationships. When you value and respect yourself, you are more likely to attract and maintain relationships with individuals who also value and respect you. This mutual respect strengthens the foundation of your relationships and promotes a sense of equality and partnership.

The Journey to Self-Love

The journey to self-love is a lifelong process that involves continuous growth, reflection, and self-discovery. It is not a destination but an ongoing commitment to yourself and your well-being. By embracing the practices and principles of self-love, you can cultivate a deeper sense of self-acceptance and care, empowering you to bring your best self to your relationships and to live a more fulfilling and meaningful life.

Embracing Impermanence

Life is constantly changing, and so are you. Embrace the impermanence of life and recognize that self-love is a dynamic process. Allow yourself to grow, evolve, and adapt to new experiences and challenges.

Practicing Gratitude

Gratitude is a powerful practice for fostering self-love. Take time to appreciate your strengths, achievements, and the positive aspects of your life. By practicing gratitude, you cultivate a sense of contentment and self-acceptance.

Seeking Support

The journey to self-love is not one you have to take alone. Seek support from friends, family, therapists, or support groups. Surround yourself with individuals who uplift and encourage you on your journey.

Continuous Learning

Self-love involves continuous learning and self-improvement. Stay curious and open to new experiences, knowledge, and perspectives. Engage in activities that promote personal growth and self-discovery.

Celebrating Yourself

Take time to celebrate yourself and your accomplishments. Acknowledge your efforts and achievements, no matter how small. By celebrating yourself, you reinforce a positive self-image and cultivate a sense of pride and self-worth.

Self-love is the foundation of all healthy relationships. It involves recognizing your worth, embracing your flaws and imperfections, and prioritizing your well-being. By cultivating self-love and self-acceptance, you empower yourself to bring your best self into your relationships, fostering deeper connections and a more fulfilling life. Embrace the journey to self-love as a continuous process of growth, reflection, and self-discovery, and commit to treating yourself with the kindness, respect, and compassion you deserve.

Chapter 13

The Romantic Paradox: Why Men Change Over Time

The beginning of a romantic relationship is often characterized by intense emotions, passion, and a sense of magic. This period, commonly known as the honeymoon phase, is filled with gestures of affection, frequent communication, and a deep sense of connection. However, many couples notice a shift in their partner's behavior as time goes on, particularly among men. This change can be perplexing and disheartening, leading to questions about the nature of romance and commitment. It explores the romantic paradox, providing insights into why men may change over time and offering strategies for maintaining romance and connection throughout the relationship.

The Honeymoon Phase: A Period of Intense Romance

The honeymoon phase is marked by heightened excitement and intense emotional connection. During this period, men often go out of their way to express their love and affection. They may engage in grand romantic gestures, frequent communication, and show an eagerness to spend time with their partner. This phase is fueled by the novelty of the relationship, the thrill of discovering a new partner, and the natural biochemical reactions in the brain associated with love and attraction. Several factors contribute to the heightened romance during the honeymoon phase

Novelty and Discovery

The excitement of getting to know someone new and the thrill of discovering shared interests, values, and goals can create a sense of magic and connection.

Biochemical Reactions: The brain releases chemicals such as dopamine, oxytocin, and serotonin, which enhance feelings of pleasure, bonding, and euphoria.

These biochemical reactions contribute to the intense emotions and behaviors observed during the honeymoon phase.

Idealization: During the initial stages of a relationship, individuals often focus on their partner's positive qualities and may idealize them. This idealization can amplify feelings of love and admiration.

The Shift: Why Men May Change Over Time

As the relationship progresses, it is natural for the intensity of the honeymoon phase to wane. This shift can be attributed to several factors, including the stabilization of biochemical reactions, the transition from novelty to familiarity, and the emergence of daily responsibilities and stressors. While the initial intensity may diminish, this does not necessarily indicate a decline in love or commitment. Understanding the reasons behind this change can help couples navigate this transition and maintain a strong and connected relationship.

Biochemical Stabilization

The brain's initial surge of chemicals stabilizes over time, leading to a decrease in the intense emotions experienced during the honeymoon phase. This stabilization is a natural part of the brain's adaptation process and does not signify a loss of love or attraction.

Transition from Novelty to Familiarity

As partners become more familiar with each other, the novelty and excitement of discovering new aspects of their partner naturally diminish. This transition to familiarity can lead to a shift in behavior and emotional intensity.

Daily Responsibilities and Stressors

The realities of daily life, including work, household responsibilities, and external stressors, can impact the dynamics of the relationship. These responsibilities may lead to a decrease in the frequency of romantic gestures and communication.

Comfort and Security

As the relationship becomes more established, partners may feel a sense of comfort and security that allows them to relax and be their authentic selves. This comfort can lead to a decrease in the need for constant validation and romantic gestures.

Maintaining Romance and Connection

While it is natural for the intensity of the honeymoon phase to decrease, it is possible to maintain romance and connection throughout the relationship. This requires conscious effort, open communication, and a commitment to nurturing the relationship. Here are several strategies for maintaining romance and connection:

Prioritize Quality Time

Make time for each other and prioritize quality time together. This can include date nights, weekend getaways, or simply spending time together at home. Quality time fosters connection and intimacy.

Practice Gratitude and Appreciation

Express gratitude and appreciation for your partner regularly. Acknowledge their efforts, strengths, and positive qualities. This practice reinforces positive feelings and fosters a sense of appreciation and love.

Keep the Romance Alive

Continue to engage in romantic gestures and activities that you enjoyed during the honeymoon phase. This can include surprise gifts, love notes, or planning special dates. These gestures keep the romance alive and show your partner that you care.

Communicate Openly

Open communication is essential for maintaining connection. Share your thoughts, feelings, and concerns with your partner. Listen actively and empathetically to your partner's perspective. Effective communication fosters understanding and intimacy.

Support Each Other's Growth

Encourage and support each other's personal growth and interests. Pursue individual passions and hobbies, and celebrate each other's achievements. Supporting each other's growth enhances the sense of partnership and mutual respect.

Practice Physical Affection

Physical affection, such as hugging, kissing, and holding hands, fosters emotional connection and intimacy. Regular physical affection strengthens the bond between partners and reinforces feelings of love and closeness.

Navigate Conflicts Constructively

Conflicts are a natural part of any relationship. Learn to navigate conflicts constructively by addressing issues calmly and respectfully. Focus on finding solutions and understanding each other's perspective. Constructive conflict resolution strengthens the relationship and fosters trust.

Cultivate Emotional Intimacy

Emotional intimacy involves sharing your innermost thoughts, feelings, and vulnerabilities with your partner. Cultivating emotional intimacy requires trust, openness, and empathy. This deep level of connection strengthens the bond between partners.

Embrace Change and Growth

Recognize that relationships evolve and change over time. Embrace this change as an opportunity for growth and deeper connection. Adapt to new circumstances and challenges together, and view them as opportunities to strengthen your relationship.

Create Shared Goals and Memories

Establish shared goals and create meaningful memories together. Whether it's planning for the future, traveling, or pursuing a shared hobby, these shared experiences enhance the sense of partnership and connection.

Understanding the Romantic Paradox

The romantic paradox refers to the observation that men can be intensely romantic initially but may change over time. Understanding this paradox involves recognizing the natural progression of relationships and the factors that influence behavior and emotional intensity. It is important to differentiate between the initial intensity of the honeymoon phase and the deeper, more enduring aspects of love and commitment.

Natural Progression

Relationships naturally evolve from the initial intensity of the honeymoon phase to a more stable and secure phase. This progression is a normal part of the relationship lifecycle and does not indicate a decline in love or commitment.

Depth of Connection

While the initial intensity may decrease, the depth of connection and emotional intimacy can grow stronger over time. This deeper connection is built on trust, understanding, and shared experiences.

Commitment and Partnership

Long-term relationships require commitment and partnership. This involves navigating challenges, supporting each other's growth, and maintaining a sense of connection and romance.

Rekindling Romance

It is possible to rekindle the romance and passion in a long-term relationship. This requires conscious effort, creativity, and a willingness to prioritize the relationship. By continuing to engage in romantic gestures and activities, couples can keep the spark alive.

The journey of maintaining romance and connection in a long-term relationship is an ongoing process that requires effort, communication, and commitment. By understanding the romantic paradox and the natural progression of relationships, couples can navigate the changes and challenges that arise over time. Embrace the journey as an opportunity for growth, deeper connection, and lasting love.

Remember that the initial intensity of the honeymoon phase is just one aspect of the relationship. The true depth and beauty of love lie in the enduring connection, trust, and partnership that develop over time. By prioritizing quality time, practicing gratitude, keeping the romance alive, communicating openly, and supporting each other's growth, couples can maintain a strong and connected relationship.

Embrace the changes and challenges as opportunities to strengthen your bond and deepen your connection. Celebrate the journey of love and commitment, and continue to nurture the romance and intimacy in your relationship. By doing so, you create a lasting and fulfilling partnership that stands the test of time.

Chapter 14

The Nice Girl Syndrome: Avoiding Being Taken for Granted

The "Nice Girl Syndrome" refers to a pattern where women, often driven by a desire to please and accommodate, end up being taken for granted in their relationships. This syndrome can lead to feelings of frustration, resentment, and low self-worth. Understanding why men may take "nice girls" for granted and learning strategies to assert your worth can help foster mutual respect and appreciation in your relationship. It focuses into the dynamics of the Nice Girl Syndrome and provides actionable insights to avoid this trap.

Understanding the Nice Girl Syndrome

The Nice Girl Syndrome is rooted in social and cultural conditioning that encourages women to be agreeable, accommodating, and self-sacrificing. While these traits can be positive in moderation, when taken to an extreme, they can lead to a lack of boundaries, suppressed needs, and an imbalance in relationships. Women who fall into this pattern often prioritize their partner's needs over their own, avoid conflict, and strive to maintain harmony at all costs. Several factors contribute to the development of the Nice Girl Syndrome

Cultural and Social Conditioning

From a young age, many women are taught to be nurturing, compliant, and selfless. These societal expectations can shape their behavior and attitudes in relationships.

Fear of Rejection

The fear of being rejected or abandoned can drive women to be overly accommodating and compliant, hoping to maintain their partner's affection and approval.

Low Self-Worth

A lack of self-confidence and low self-esteem can lead women to believe that they must earn love and acceptance by being overly nice and self-sacrificing.

Desire for Approval

The need for external validation and approval can make women more likely to prioritize others' needs over their own.

The Impact of Being Taken for Granted

When women fall into the Nice Girl Syndrome, they may find themselves being taken for granted by their partners. This can manifest in various ways, such as a lack of appreciation, unequal distribution of responsibilities, and a sense of being undervalued. Over time, this dynamic can erode the foundation of the relationship, leading to feelings of resentment and dissatisfaction.

Lack of Appreciation

When a woman is consistently accommodating and self-sacrificing, her efforts may go unnoticed or unappreciated by her partner. This lack of appreciation can lead to feelings of invisibility and undervaluation.

Unequal Distribution of Responsibilities

In relationships where one partner is overly accommodating, the distribution of responsibilities may become unbalanced. This can result in one partner shouldering the majority of the emotional and practical burdens, leading to burnout and resentment.

Erosion of Self-Worth

Being taken for granted can erode a woman's self-worth and confidence. She may begin to doubt her value and question whether she deserves better treatment.

Resentment and Frustration

Over time, the imbalance and lack of appreciation can lead to deep-seated resentment and frustration. This can strain the relationship and create emotional distance between partners.

Strategies to Assert Your Worth

Avoiding the Nice Girl Syndrome and asserting your worth involves developing self-awareness, setting boundaries, and cultivating self-respect. By taking proactive steps to prioritize your needs and assert your value, you can foster mutual respect and appreciation in your relationship.

Cultivate Self-Awareness

Developing self-awareness is the first step in recognizing patterns of behavior that contribute to the Nice Girl Syndrome. Reflect on your actions and motivations in the relationship. Are you prioritizing your partner's needs at the expense of your own? Are you afraid to express your true feelings or desires? Understanding these patterns can help you make conscious changes.

Set Healthy Boundaries

Setting and maintaining healthy boundaries is essential for asserting your worth. Boundaries protect your well-being and ensure that your needs are respected. Identify your limits and communicate them clearly to your partner. For example, if you need time for self-care, make it known and prioritize it. Boundaries create a sense of balance and mutual respect in the relationship.

Practice Self-Care

Prioritize self-care and make time for activities that nurture your physical, emotional, and mental well-being. Self-care is not selfish; it is a vital practice for maintaining your overall health and happiness. Engage in activities that bring you joy, relaxation, and fulfillment. By taking care of yourself, you demonstrate self-respect and reinforce your worth.

Communicate Assertively

Effective communication is key to asserting your worth and avoiding being taken for granted. Practice assertive communication, which involves expressing your thoughts, feelings, and needs clearly and respectfully. Use "I" statements to convey your perspective without blaming or criticizing your partner. For example, say, "I feel unappreciated when my efforts go unnoticed. I would like more recognition and gratitude."

Recognize and Challenge Negative Beliefs

Identify and challenge negative beliefs that contribute to the Nice Girl Syndrome. These beliefs may include thoughts such as "I must always please others to be loved" or "My needs are not as important as my partner's." Replace these negative beliefs with positive affirmations that reinforce your worth and value. For example, affirm, "I deserve to have my needs met" and "My well-being is important."

Seek Support

Surround yourself with supportive friends, family, or a therapist who can provide encouragement and validation. Talking to others who understand and appreciate you can boost your confidence and reinforce your sense of worth. Seeking support also provides a safe space to explore your feelings and gain insights into your relationship dynamics.

Foster Mutual Respect

Cultivate a relationship based on mutual respect and appreciation. Show gratitude for your partner's efforts and express appreciation for their positive qualities. Encourage your partner to reciprocate by acknowledging and valuing your contributions. Mutual respect creates a balanced and healthy dynamic in the relationship.

Embrace Your Authentic Self

Embrace and express your authentic self without fear of judgment or rejection. Authenticity fosters genuine connections and deepens intimacy in relationships. Allow yourself to be vulnerable and share your true thoughts, feelings, and desires with your partner. By being true to yourself, you reinforce your worth and create a foundation of trust and respect.

Overcoming the Fear of Rejection

The fear of rejection is a significant barrier to asserting your worth and avoiding the Nice Girl Syndrome. Overcoming this fear involves developing self-confidence and self-compassion. Recognize that your worth is not determined by others' opinions or approval. You are inherently valuable and deserving of love and respect.

Build Self-Confidence

Build self-confidence by setting and achieving personal goals, celebrating your accomplishments, and recognizing your strengths. Confidence empowers you to assert your worth and stand up for your needs.

Practice Self-Compassion

Practice self-compassion by treating yourself with kindness and understanding, especially during times of struggle or failure. Self-compassion fosters resilience and reinforces your sense of worth.

Challenge the Fear of Rejection

Challenge the fear of rejection by reframing it as an opportunity for growth and learning. Recognize that rejection is a natural part of life and relationships. It does not diminish your value or worth. Embrace rejection as a stepping stone to personal growth and self-discovery.

Building a Balanced and Respectful Relationship

Creating a balanced and respectful relationship involves continuous effort and commitment from both partners. It requires open communication, mutual appreciation, and a willingness to grow together. By fostering a relationship based on equality and respect, you can avoid the Nice Girl Syndrome and create a fulfilling and lasting partnership.

Encourage Open Communication

Foster an environment of open and honest communication. Encourage your partner to share their thoughts and feelings, and actively listen to their perspective. Open communication enhances understanding and connection.

Practice Mutual Appreciation

Regularly express appreciation for each other's efforts and contributions. Acknowledge the small and big things your partner does to make the relationship work. Mutual appreciation fosters a sense of gratitude and respect.

Share Responsibilities

Ensure that responsibilities are shared equitably in the relationship. Collaborate on household tasks, financial responsibilities, and emotional support. Sharing responsibilities creates a sense of partnership and balance.

Support Each Other's Growth

Encourage and support each other's personal growth and development. Celebrate each other's achievements and provide encouragement during challenges. Supporting each other's growth strengthens the bond and fosters mutual respect.

Cultivate Emotional Intimacy

Invest in cultivating emotional intimacy by sharing your innermost thoughts, feelings, and vulnerabilities. Emotional intimacy deepens the connection and fosters a sense of trust and understanding.

The Nice Girl Syndrome can be a challenging pattern to overcome, but with self-awareness, assertiveness, and a commitment to self-respect, it is possible to create a balanced and respectful relationship. Recognize your inherent worth and prioritize your well-being. Set healthy boundaries, communicate assertively, and practice self-care. Foster mutual respect and appreciation in your relationship, and embrace your authentic self.

Remember that you deserve to be valued, respected, and appreciated in your relationships. By asserting your worth and avoiding the Nice Girl Syndrome, you can create a fulfilling and lasting partnership based on equality, respect, and love. Embrace the journey of self-discovery and self-empowerment, and celebrate the unique and valuable person that you are.

Chapter 15

Earning Respect: The Strength of Standing Up for Yourself

Respect is the cornerstone of any healthy relationship. It fosters trust, appreciation, and mutual understanding. However, earning respect, especially in romantic relationships, often requires assertiveness and the courage to stand up for oneself. This explores why men respect women who assert their boundaries and how to command that respect by maintaining dignity in all interactions. By understanding the dynamics of respect and learning practical strategies to assert yourself, you can create a balanced and empowering relationship.

The Importance of Respect in Relationships

Respect is fundamental to the health and longevity of any relationship. It involves recognizing and valuing each other's boundaries, needs, and individuality. When respect is present, partners feel valued, understood, and secure. It creates an environment where both individuals can thrive and grow together.

Fosters Trust and Security

Respect fosters trust and security in a relationship. When partners respect each other, they feel safe to express their true selves without fear of judgment or rejection.

Enhances Communication

Respectful interactions enhance communication by encouraging open and honest dialogue. It allows partners to listen actively and understand each other's perspectives.

Promotes Equality

Respect promotes equality by acknowledging each partner's value and contributions. It ensures that both individuals feel empowered and appreciated.

Strengthens Emotional Connection

Respect strengthens the emotional connection between partners. It creates a sense of mutual understanding and empathy, deepening the bond.

Why Men Respect Women Who Stand Up for Themselves

Men, like anyone, value and respect individuals who assert their boundaries and stand up for themselves. This behavior demonstrates self-worth, confidence, and strength. When a woman stands up for herself, it signals that she values her dignity and will not tolerate disrespect.

Self-Worth and Confidence

A woman who stands up for herself exudes self-worth and confidence. This self-assurance is attractive and commands respect. It shows that she knows her value and will not settle for less.

Boundaries and Limits

Setting boundaries and limits is a sign of self-respect. It communicates that she will not allow others to take advantage of her. Men respect women who establish and maintain boundaries because it shows that they have a clear sense of self and are not afraid to protect their well-being.

Assertiveness and Strength

Assertiveness is the ability to express one's needs, desires, and boundaries clearly and confidently. It is a sign of strength and independence. Men respect women who are assertive because it demonstrates that they are capable of standing up for themselves and will not be easily swayed.

Authenticity and Integrity

Standing up for oneself requires authenticity and integrity. It involves being true to one's values and beliefs. Men respect women who are authentic and maintain their integrity, as it shows that they are genuine and trustworthy.

Strategies to Command Respect

Earning respect involves more than just demanding it; it requires consistent actions and behaviors that demonstrate self-respect and dignity. By employing these strategies, you can command respect and create a balanced and empowering relationship.

Develop Self-Awareness

Self-awareness is the foundation of earning respect. Understand your values, needs, and boundaries. Reflect on your strengths and areas for growth. Self-awareness allows you to assert yourself confidently and authentically.

Set Clear Boundaries

Establish clear boundaries and communicate them to your partner. Boundaries protect your well-being and ensure that your needs are respected. Be consistent in enforcing your boundaries and do not be afraid to assert them when necessary.

Practice Assertive Communication

Assertive communication involves expressing your thoughts, feelings, and needs clearly and respectfully. Use "I" statements to convey your perspective without blaming or criticizing your partner. For example, say, "I feel disrespected when my boundaries are not acknowledged. I need you to respect my limits."

Maintain Integrity

Stay true to your values and beliefs, even in the face of pressure or opposition. Integrity involves being honest and authentic in your interactions. When you maintain your integrity, you demonstrate that you are reliable and trustworthy.

Show Self-Respect

Demonstrate self-respect through your actions and behaviors. Take care of your physical, emotional, and mental well-being. Make choices that align with your values and priorities. When you respect yourself, others are more likely to respect you.

Stand Firm in Your Decisions

Once you have made a decision based on your values and boundaries, stand firm in it. Do not allow others to sway you or undermine your choices. Firmness in your decisions shows that you are confident and unwavering in your principles.

Seek Mutual Respect

Foster an environment of mutual respect in your relationship. Show respect to your partner and encourage them to do the same. Mutual respect creates a balanced and healthy dynamic where both partners feel valued and appreciated.

Address Disrespect Immediately

If you encounter disrespect in your relationship, address it immediately. Communicate your feelings and set clear expectations for future behavior. Do not tolerate disrespect or allow it to go unchecked.

Overcoming Challenges to Standing Up for Yourself

Standing up for yourself can be challenging, especially if you have been conditioned to prioritize others' needs over your own. Overcoming these challenges involves developing self-confidence, challenging negative beliefs, and seeking support.

Build Self-Confidence

Confidence is key to standing up for yourself. Build self-confidence by setting and achieving personal goals, celebrating your accomplishments, and recognizing your strengths. Confidence empowers you to assert your boundaries and command respect.

Challenge Negative Beliefs

Identify and challenge negative beliefs that undermine your self-worth. These beliefs may include thoughts such as "I am not important" or "I must please others to be loved." Replace these negative beliefs with positive affirmations that reinforce your worth and value. For example, affirm, "I am worthy of respect" and "My needs are important."

Seek Support

Surround yourself with supportive friends, family, or a therapist who can provide encouragement and validation. Talking to others who understand and appreciate you can boost your confidence and reinforce your sense of worth. Seeking support also provides a safe space to explore your feelings and gain insights into your relationship dynamics.

Practice Self-Compassion

Practice self-compassion by treating yourself with kindness and understanding, especially during times of struggle or failure. Self-compassion fosters resilience and reinforces your sense of worth. It allows you to stand up for yourself without fear of judgment or rejection.

Develop Conflict Resolution Skills

Effective conflict resolution skills are essential for standing up for yourself in a respectful and constructive manner. Learn to address conflicts calmly and assertively. Focus on finding solutions and understanding each other's perspectives. Constructive conflict resolution strengthens the relationship and fosters mutual respect.

The Benefits of Standing Up for Yourself

Standing up for yourself has numerous benefits for both you and your relationship. It enhances your self-worth, fosters mutual respect, and creates a balanced and empowering dynamic.

Enhanced Self-Worth

Asserting your boundaries and standing up for yourself enhances your self-worth and confidence. It reinforces the belief that you are valuable and deserving of respect.

Mutual Respect

When you stand up for yourself, you encourage mutual respect in your relationship. It sets a standard for how you expect to be treated and shows your partner that you value yourself.

Balanced Relationship Dynamics

Standing up for yourself creates a balanced dynamic where both partners feel empowered and appreciated. It ensures that your needs are considered and respected, fostering a healthier and more fulfilling relationship.

Strengthened Emotional Connection

Asserting your boundaries and maintaining dignity fosters a deeper emotional connection. It creates an environment of trust, understanding, and empathy, strengthening the bond between partners.

Empowerment and Independence

Standing up for yourself empowers you to take control of your life and relationship. It promotes independence and self-reliance, allowing you to thrive as an individual and as a partner.

Earning respect and standing up for yourself is a journey of self-discovery and empowerment. By developing self-awareness, setting clear boundaries, practicing assertive communication, and maintaining integrity, you can command respect and create a balanced and empowering relationship.

Remember that you are inherently valuable and deserving of respect. Embrace your strength and dignity, and do not be afraid to assert your worth. By standing up for yourself, you foster mutual respect and appreciation in your relationship, creating a foundation of trust, understanding, and love.

Celebrate your journey of self-empowerment and continue to prioritize your well-being and self-respect. By doing so, you create a fulfilling and lasting partnership where both you and your partner can thrive and grow together. Embrace your worth and command the respect you deserve.

Chapter 16

Identifying Red Flags: Spotting Potential Pitfalls and Toxic Behaviors

In any relationship, it's essential to be aware of behaviors and patterns that may indicate underlying issues or potential toxicity. Recognizing red flags early on can save you from emotional distress and help you make informed decisions about the future of your relationship. It provides you with the tools to identify red flags, understand their implications, and take proactive steps to ensure your well-being and happiness.

Understanding Red Flags and Their Importance

Red flags are warning signs that something may be wrong in a relationship. They can range from subtle behaviors to overt actions that indicate potential problems. Recognizing these signs is crucial because they can escalate over time, leading to more significant issues and emotional harm.

Early Detection

Spotting red flags early allows you to address issues before they become deeply entrenched. It gives you the opportunity to discuss concerns with your partner and decide whether the relationship is worth pursuing.

Protecting Your Well-being

Identifying red flags helps you protect your emotional, mental, and physical well-being. It ensures that you do not invest in a relationship that may cause harm or lead to unhealthy dynamics.

Empowerment

Being aware of red flags empowers you to make informed decisions about your relationships. It allows you to set boundaries and take control of your life, ensuring that you are treated with respect and dignity.

Common Red Flags in Relationships

Red flags can manifest in various forms and may not always be immediately apparent. Here are some common red flags to be mindful of in relationships:

Lack of Communication

Effective communication is the foundation of any healthy relationship. A partner who avoids or dismisses open and honest communication may be hiding something or unwilling to address issues constructively.

Controlling Behavior

Controlling behavior is a significant red flag. This can include monitoring your activities, dictating who you can spend time with, and making decisions for you. Such behavior undermines your autonomy and can escalate into more severe forms of control and manipulation.

Disrespect and Criticism

Consistent disrespect, belittling, or criticism can erode your self-esteem and create a toxic environment. A partner who frequently makes you feel inadequate or unworthy is not fostering a healthy relationship dynamic.

Jealousy and Possessiveness

While a certain degree of jealousy is natural, excessive jealousy and possessiveness are red flags. These behaviors indicate insecurity and a lack of trust, which can lead to controlling and abusive actions.

Lack of Support

A healthy relationship involves mutual support and encouragement. A partner who does not support your goals, dreams, and personal growth may be more focused on their own needs and less invested in your well-being.

Isolation

A partner who tries to isolate you from friends, family, or other support networks is exhibiting a red flag behavior. Isolation can lead to dependency and make it harder for you to leave an unhealthy relationship.

Inconsistency and Unreliability

Consistent inconsistency and unreliability can indicate a lack of commitment and respect. A partner who frequently breaks promises or is unreliable in their actions may not be trustworthy or dependable.

Emotional Manipulation

Emotional manipulation includes tactics such as guilt-tripping, gaslighting, and playing the victim. These behaviors can distort your perception of reality and make you question your own feelings and experiences.

Refusal to Compromise

Relationships require compromise and collaboration. A partner who is unwilling to meet you halfway or insists on having things their way all the time may be demonstrating a lack of respect for your needs and desires.

Excessive Anger and Aggression

Frequent outbursts of anger, aggression, or hostility are major red flags. Such behavior can be indicative of deeper issues and can potentially escalate into emotional or physical abuse.

Recognizing Subtle Red Flags

Not all red flags are overt or easy to spot. Some may be subtle and require careful observation and self-awareness. Here are some subtle red flags to be aware of:

Unequal Effort

A relationship should involve equal effort from both partners. If you find yourself consistently putting in more effort, time, and energy than your partner, it may indicate an imbalance in commitment and investment.

Lack of Empathy

Empathy is crucial for understanding and connecting with your partner. A lack of empathy or indifference to your feelings and experiences can be a subtle red flag indicating emotional distance or selfishness.

Inconsistent Behavior

Pay attention to patterns of inconsistent behavior. A partner who is warm and loving one moment and distant or cold the next may be unreliable or emotionally unstable.

Secretive Behavior

Secrecy and a lack of transparency can be red flags. If your partner is overly secretive about their activities, communication, or past, it may indicate a lack of trustworthiness or hidden issues.

Dismissive Attitude

A partner who consistently dismisses your concerns, feelings, or opinions is not showing respect or valuing your perspective. This dismissive attitude can undermine your self-worth and create a toxic dynamic.

Tools for Identifying and Addressing Red Flags

Recognizing red flags is the first step; addressing them is equally important. Here are some tools to help you identify and address red flags in your relationship:

Self-Reflection

Regular self-reflection helps you understand your own feelings, needs, and boundaries. Take time to assess your relationship and identify any red flags that may be present.

Open Communication

Communicate openly and honestly with your partner about your concerns. Use "I" statements to express how certain behaviors make you feel and discuss potential solutions.

Seek Support

Reach out to trusted friends, family, or a therapist for support and guidance. They can provide an outside perspective and help you navigate difficult situations.

Set Boundaries

Establish and enforce clear boundaries to protect your well-being. Communicate your boundaries to your partner and be firm in maintaining them.

Trust Your Instincts

Trust your instincts and intuition. If something feels off or makes you uncomfortable, pay attention to those feelings and investigate further.

Observe Patterns

Look for patterns of behavior over time. Isolated incidents may not always be red flags, but consistent patterns can indicate deeper issues.

Prioritize Self-Care

Prioritize your physical, emotional, and mental well-being. Engage in activities that bring you joy and relaxation, and take care of yourself.

Educate Yourself

Educate yourself about healthy relationship dynamics and toxic behaviors. The more you know, the better equipped you will be to identify and address red flags.

Making Informed Decisions

Once you have identified red flags, it's important to make informed decisions about your relationship. Here are some steps to help you navigate this process:

Assess the Severity

Assess the severity of the red flags you have identified. Are they isolated incidents or part of a consistent pattern? Consider the impact they have on your well-being and the overall health of the relationship.

Discuss with Your Partner

Have an open and honest discussion with your partner about your concerns. Share specific examples of the behaviors you have noticed and express how they make you feel. Listen to their perspective and see if they are willing to acknowledge and address the issues.

Set Expectations

Set clear expectations for behavior and communication moving forward. Discuss what changes are needed to create a healthier dynamic and how you both can work towards achieving them.

Monitor Progress

Monitor the progress of the changes you have discussed. Are the red flags being addressed and resolved? Is your partner making a genuine effort to improve the relationship?

Consider Professional Help

If the red flags persist or if you feel overwhelmed, consider seeking professional help. A therapist or relationship counselor can provide valuable insights and strategies to navigate the challenges.

Prioritize Your Well-being

Ultimately, prioritize your well-being and happiness. If the red flags continue to persist and negatively impact your life, it may be necessary to reevaluate the relationship and consider whether it is in your best interest to stay.

Empowering Yourself with Knowledge and Awareness

Identifying red flags and potential pitfalls in relationships is a crucial skill that empowers you to make informed decisions and protect your well-being. By being aware of common red flags, recognizing subtle signs, and using the tools provided in this chapter, you can navigate your relationships with confidence and clarity.

Remember that you deserve to be in a relationship where you are treated with respect, kindness, and love. Do not ignore red flags or dismiss your feelings. Trust yourself and prioritize your well-being. By doing so, you can create healthy, fulfilling relationships that support your growth and happiness.

Empower yourself with knowledge and awareness, and take proactive steps to ensure that your relationships are positive and nurturing. You have the strength and wisdom to identify red flags, address issues, and make decisions that honor your worth and dignity. Embrace this journey of self-awareness and relationship empowerment, and build the loving, respectful relationships you deserve.

Chapter 17

Building Healthy Relationships: Creating Fulfilling Partnerships

Building a healthy relationship is an intricate yet rewarding endeavor that involves commitment, effort, and a deep understanding of mutual respect and love. This looks into the essential elements of creating fulfilling partnerships, providing you with a comprehensive guide to nurture lasting, happy relationships.

The Foundation of Healthy Relationships

At the core of every healthy relationship lies a foundation built on key principles such as trust, communication, respect, and love. These elements are crucial for establishing a solid base upon which a thriving relationship can grow.

Trust

Trust is the bedrock of any healthy relationship. It involves being reliable, honest, and consistent. Trust allows partners to feel secure and confident in each other, fostering a safe and stable environment.

Communication

Open and honest communication is essential for understanding each other's needs, desires, and concerns. It enables partners to express themselves freely, resolve conflicts effectively, and build a deeper connection.

Respect

Mutual respect is vital for a healthy relationship. It involves valuing each other's opinions, boundaries, and individuality. Respect ensures that both partners feel appreciated and honored, creating a positive dynamic.

Love

Love encompasses affection, care, and emotional intimacy. It is the emotional glue that binds partners together, providing comfort, support, and a sense of belonging.

Building Emotional Intimacy

Emotional intimacy is the heart of a fulfilling relationship. It involves sharing your innermost thoughts, feelings, and experiences with your partner, creating a deep and meaningful connection.

Vulnerability

Being vulnerable means opening up and sharing your true self with your partner. It requires trust and courage but fosters a deeper emotional bond. Share your fears, dreams, and insecurities to build a stronger connection.

Empathy

Empathy involves understanding and validating your partner's emotions. It means putting yourself in their shoes and responding with compassion. Practicing empathy strengthens your emotional connection and promotes a supportive environment.

Active Listening

Active listening is a crucial skill for emotional intimacy. It involves fully focusing on your partner, understanding their message, and responding thoughtfully. Avoid interrupting or judging, and show genuine interest in their thoughts and feelings.

Quality Time

Spending quality time together helps nurture emotional intimacy. Engage in activities that you both enjoy, have meaningful conversations, and create shared experiences. Prioritize time together to strengthen your bond.

Effective Communication Strategies

Effective communication is the cornerstone of a healthy relationship. It involves not only expressing your thoughts and feelings but also understanding and responding to your partner's communication style.

Assertiveness

Assertive communication involves expressing your needs and boundaries clearly and respectfully. Use "I" statements to convey your feelings without blaming or accusing your partner.

Nonverbal Communication

Pay attention to nonverbal cues such as body language, facial expressions, and tone of voice. Nonverbal communication can convey emotions and intentions, providing deeper insights into your partner's feelings.

Conflict Resolution

Conflicts are inevitable in any relationship, but how you handle them can make a significant difference. Approach conflicts with a problem-solving mindset, avoid blame, and focus on finding mutually beneficial solutions.

Affirmation

Positive affirmations and expressions of gratitude can strengthen your relationship. Regularly acknowledge and appreciate your partner's efforts, qualities, and contributions.

Maintaining Mutual Respect

Mutual respect is fundamental for a healthy relationship. It involves valuing each other's individuality, boundaries, and contributions.

Recognize Individuality

Celebrate and respect each other's individuality. Encourage personal growth and pursuits, and avoid trying to change your partner. Embrace each other's unique qualities and differences.

Set Boundaries

Establish and respect each other's boundaries. Boundaries protect your personal space and well-being, ensuring that both partners feel safe and respected.

Equality and Fairness

Strive for equality and fairness in your relationship. Make decisions together, share responsibilities, and avoid power imbalances. Treat each other as equals, with mutual respect and consideration.

Support and Encouragement

Provide unwavering support and encouragement for each other's goals and dreams. Celebrate successes together and offer comfort during challenges. Be each other's biggest cheerleader.

Cultivating Shared Goals and Values

Shared goals and values form the foundation for a united and harmonious relationship. They provide a sense of purpose and direction, fostering a deeper connection and commitment.

Aligning Values

Discuss and align your core values and beliefs. Identify the principles that are most important to both of you and ensure that they are in harmony. Shared values create a strong foundation for your relationship.

Setting Goals Together

Set both short-term and long-term goals together. Whether it's planning a future trip, buying a home, or starting a family, having shared goals fosters teamwork and collaboration.

Creating Traditions

Establishing traditions and rituals can strengthen your bond and create lasting memories. Whether it's a weekly date night, holiday traditions, or special celebrations, shared traditions enhance your connection.

Building a Future

Plan and build a future together. Discuss your dreams, aspirations, and vision for the future. Work together to create a life that aligns with both of your desires and ambitions.

Maintaining Romance and Passion

Romance and passion are essential for keeping the spark alive in your relationship. They add excitement, intimacy, and joy, creating a fulfilling partnership.

Express Affection

Regularly express affection through physical touch, words of affirmation, and loving gestures. Small acts of affection, such as holding hands, hugging, or saying "I love you," can make a big difference.

Keep the Spark Alive

Continuously find ways to keep the romance alive. Plan surprise dates, write love notes, or create special moments together. Keep the excitement and passion alive by prioritizing each other.

Intimacy and Connection

Nurture intimacy and connection through regular physical and emotional closeness. Engage in activities that strengthen your bond, such as cuddling, talking, or spending quality time together.

Spontaneity

Embrace spontaneity and adventure in your relationship. Try new activities, explore new places, or take spontaneous trips together. Keep the relationship exciting and fresh.

Navigating Challenges Together

Every relationship faces challenges, but how you navigate them can determine the strength and resilience of your partnership. Approach challenges with a united front and a problem-solving mindset.

Teamwork

Approach challenges as a team. Work together to find solutions, support each other, and overcome obstacles. Emphasize collaboration and mutual support.

Adaptability

Be adaptable and flexible in your relationship. Life is unpredictable, and being able to adapt to changes and challenges strengthens your bond.

Forgiveness and Understanding

Practice forgiveness and understanding. Everyone makes mistakes, and holding onto grudges can damage your relationship. Focus on resolving issues and moving forward with a positive outlook.

Seek Help When Needed

Don't hesitate to seek professional help if needed. A therapist or counselor can provide valuable insights and strategies to navigate challenges and strengthen your relationship.

Creating Fulfilling Partnerships

Building a healthy relationship requires dedication, effort, and a deep understanding of mutual respect and love. By focusing on trust, communication, respect, and love, you can create a solid foundation for a thriving partnership. Nurture emotional intimacy, practice effective communication, and maintain mutual respect to strengthen your bond.

Cultivate shared goals and values, keep the romance and passion alive, and navigate challenges together to build a fulfilling partnership. Remember that a healthy relationship is a continuous journey of growth, understanding, and mutual support. Embrace this journey with an open heart and a commitment to creating a loving, respectful, and fulfilling partnership.

By following the guidance in this chapter, you can create a relationship that brings joy, fulfillment, and lasting happiness. Celebrate the beauty of healthy relationships and the profound impact they have on your life. You deserve to experience the love and connection that come from building a strong, fulfilling partnership based on mutual respect and love.

Conclusion

The journey through understanding and cultivating strong, independent, and fulfilling relationships has brought us to a place of profound self-awareness and insight. This conclusion aims to encapsulate the essence of what we've explored, providing a final, comprehensive guide to embracing and implementing the principles discussed.

Independence and self-sufficiency are not merely attributes but cornerstones of a fulfilling life and relationship. Throughout this book, we've highlighted the importance of cultivating these qualities. Independence does not mean isolation; rather, it means having the confidence and strength to stand on your own while still cherishing the bonds you create with others.

Self-sufficiency empowers you to meet your own needs and find happiness within yourself. This inner contentment radiates outward, attracting partners who appreciate and respect your autonomy. By embracing independence, you ensure that your relationships are based on mutual respect and genuine connection rather than dependency.

Self-love is the foundation upon which all healthy relationships are built. It involves accepting yourself fully, with all your strengths and imperfections. This journey of self-acceptance is ongoing and requires patience and compassion. When you love and respect yourself, you set the standard for how others should treat you.

Personal growth is a lifelong journey. Pursuing your passions and interests enriches your life and enhances your relationships. It allows you to bring your best self into your partnerships, fostering a dynamic where both individuals can grow and thrive together. By continuously working on personal development, you create a fulfilling and evolving relationship.

Effective communication is the lifeblood of any relationship. It involves more than just talking; it requires active listening, empathy, and clarity. Through open and honest communication, you build trust and understanding with your partner. This book has provided various strategies for enhancing your communication skills, emphasizing the importance of both verbal and nonverbal cues.

Setting and maintaining healthy boundaries is crucial for preserving your well-being and the health of your relationship. Boundaries protect your personal space and ensure that your needs are respected. They foster a sense of security and mutual respect, allowing both partners to feel valued and understood. By clearly defining and communicating your boundaries, you create a balanced and harmonious dynamic.

The dynamics of male-female interactions are complex and multifaceted. Understanding these dynamics helps you navigate your relationships more effectively. Attraction is often rooted in qualities such as confidence, independence, and self-assurance. Men are drawn to strong women because they exude these qualities, creating a sense of intrigue and admiration.

This book has explored the psychology of attraction, shedding light on why confident and self-assured women are so appealing. By embodying these traits, you not only attract partners who appreciate and respect you but also cultivate a relationship based on equality and mutual respect.

Every relationship faces challenges, but it is how you navigate these obstacles that determines the strength and resilience of your partnership. Approaching challenges with a problem-solving mindset and a united front fosters a supportive and collaborative environment.

Embracing vulnerability is key to building emotional intimacy. It involves opening up and sharing your true self with your partner. While vulnerability requires courage, it strengthens your bond and deepens your connection. By being vulnerable, you create a space where both partners can be authentic and honest, fostering a deeper understanding and empathy.

Romance and passion are vital for keeping the spark alive in your relationship. They add excitement, intimacy, and joy, creating a fulfilling partnership. This book has provided various strategies for nurturing romantic chemistry, emphasizing the importance of regular expressions of affection, spontaneity, and quality time together.

Maintaining romance and passion requires effort and creativity. It involves finding new ways to connect and keeping the excitement alive. By prioritizing your relationship and making time for each other, you ensure that the romance continues to flourish.

Recognizing red flags and potential pitfalls is crucial for protecting your well-being and ensuring that your relationships are healthy. This book has highlighted common red flags and provided tools for identifying and addressing them. By being aware of these warning signs, you can make informed decisions about your relationships.

Avoiding toxic relationships involves setting clear boundaries, trusting your instincts, and prioritizing your well-being. It requires self-awareness and the courage to walk away from situations that do not serve you. By recognizing and addressing red flags early on, you protect yourself from emotional harm and create space for healthy, fulfilling relationships.

Building a strong support network is essential for navigating the complexities of relationships and personal growth. Surrounding yourself with friends, family, and mentors who support and encourage you provides a sense of security and belonging. This support network can offer valuable insights, advice, and comfort during challenging times.

Seeking professional help when needed is also crucial. A therapist or relationship counselor can provide guidance and strategies for navigating difficult situations and improving your relationship dynamics. By reaching out for help, you demonstrate a commitment to your well-being and the health of your relationships.

Mutual respect and equality are fundamental principles of a healthy relationship. They involve valuing each other's individuality, contributions, and boundaries. This book has emphasized the importance of creating a balanced dynamic where both partners feel appreciated and honored.

Fostering mutual respect requires ongoing effort and communication. It involves recognizing and celebrating each other's strengths and supporting each other's growth. By prioritizing equality and fairness, you create a partnership that is built on mutual admiration and respect.

Building a healthy and fulfilling relationship is a continuous journey. It involves ongoing effort, self-awareness, and a commitment to growth. This book has provided a comprehensive guide to navigating this journey, offering insights and strategies for creating lasting, happy partnerships.

As you move forward, remember that the principles discussed in this book are not one-time solutions but ongoing practices. Continuously work on self-love, personal growth, effective communication, and mutual respect. Embrace vulnerability, maintain romance and passion, and recognize red flags early on.

Embracing Love and Connection

Love and connection are at the heart of human experience. Building healthy relationships based on mutual respect and love enriches your life and brings joy and fulfillment. By embracing the principles discussed in this book, you create a solid foundation for lasting, happy partnerships.

Remember that you deserve to be in a relationship where you are valued, respected, and loved. Trust yourself and your journey, and never settle for anything less than a relationship that brings out the best in you. Celebrate your independence, nurture your personal growth, and build connections that honor your worth and dignity.

Know that you have the strength and wisdom to create the relationships you desire. Embrace the beauty of love and connection, and cherish the moments of joy and intimacy that come with a fulfilling partnership. You have the power to build and sustain relationships that bring happiness and meaning to your life.

The path to building healthy, fulfilling relationships is not always easy, but it is undoubtedly worth it. The insights and strategies shared in this book are meant to empower you with the knowledge and tools needed to navigate the complexities of love and partnership.

Take time to reflect on the lessons learned and the progress made. Celebrate your growth and the positive changes in your relationships. Remember that every step taken towards building a healthy relationship is a step towards a happier and more fulfilling life.

Continue to invest in yourself and your relationships, knowing that you have the ability to create the love and connection you deserve. Embrace the journey with an open heart, and let the principles of mutual respect, love, and understanding guide you towards a future filled with happiness and fulfillment.

Building healthy relationships requires a deep commitment to self-awareness, growth, and mutual respect. By embracing the principles discussed in this book, you create a foundation for lasting, happy partnerships. Celebrate your independence, nurture your personal growth, and build connections that honor your worth and dignity. Remember that you have the strength and wisdom to create the relationships you desire. Embrace the beauty of love and connection, and cherish the moments of joy and intimacy that come with a fulfilling partnership. You have the power to build and sustain relationships that bring happiness and meaning to your life.

www.ingramcontent.com/pod-product-compliance
Lightning Source LLC
Chambersburg PA
CBHW071915210526
45479CB00002B/430